Turning Trauma Into Triumph

Ten Stories of Hope and Growth, Including My Own

Turning Trauma Into Triumph

Ten Stories of Hope and Growth, Including My Own

RICHARD C. SCHEINBERG, LCSW, BCD

AuthorHouse™
1663 Liberty Drive, Suite 200
Bloomington, IN 47403
www.authorhouse.com
Phone: 1-800-839-8640

AuthorHouse™ UK Ltd.
500 Avebury Boulevard
Central Milton Keynes, MK9 2BE
www.authorhouse.co.uk
Phone: 08001974150

This book is a work of non-fiction. Unless otherwise noted, the author
and the publisher make no explicit guarantees as to the accuracy of
the information contained in this book and in some cases, names
of people and places have been altered to protect their privacy.

First published by AuthorHouse 4/11/2007

ISBN: 978-1-4259-8688-9 (sc)

Printed in the United States of America
Bloomington, Indiana

This book is printed on acid-free paper.

Interior layout and cover design by the Legwork Team.

Bloomington, IN Milton Keynes, UK

authorHOUSE™

Dedication

*My deepest love and appreciation goes to Gerry,
who has been my supportive wife for 29 years and my
best friend for more than thirty-six years.*

*A world of gratitude belongs to my son, Jared,
who gave me the chance to be the father I never had.
Also, his kindness and sensitivity show that he is an
"old soul" ready to add new light to our world.*

Acknowledgments

My heartfelt admiration goes to all the clients who have shared their lives with me. I consider their openness and trust to be emotional gifts that I am privileged to receive. My clients are an ongoing source of inspiration.

I am forever thankful to Carmine Angrisani and Myra Fischman, who were available to me at the worst of times, who spent many hours helping me to cope in the midst of my emotional chaos and who helped me discover all the blessings in my life.

I am forever grateful to Laura Berhalter, who spent most of her Sunday evenings with me for two years in order to get my thoughts and words onto paper as she typed several working drafts of this book.

Judy Gitenstein's suggestions and editing were most valuable. And finally, Yvonne Kamerling and Janet Yudewitz of the Legwork Team were very helpful in preparing the final draft of this book for publication.

A Note to the Reader

Psychotherapist-client confidentiality is a strong and time-honored principle of practice ethics. Therefore, the names and certain identifying details of the clients mentioned in this book have been altered in order to protect their privacy.

Table of Contents

INTRODUCTION

Lessons We Learn as Babies.. 10

I'm Crazy Enough to Think There's a Solution to Every Problem............... 16

We All Have the Same Issues—More or Less 30

Your Personal Connection to the Power of Spirit 33

SECTION ONE: GROWING UP

1 *Yvonne:*
Being a Child, Feeling Alone, Then Learning to Trust........................... 37

2 *Carol:*
Growing Up the Perfect Child and Discovering
Your True Self as a Wife and Mother 48

3 *Therese:*
Growing Up With Sexual Abuse, Then Learning to
Enjoy Sex and Forgive Your Past 57

4 *Paula:*
Being Sexually Violated, and Then Finding Your Power....................... 79

5 *Lenny:*
Trauma...Finding Reassurance after 9/11 98

SECTION TWO: FINDING LOVE

6 *Patti and Brett:*
When the Honeymoon Ends in Three Months.
Re-Igniting the Spark of Passion.. 103

7 *Diana:*
Love Taps...Reacting Sooner than Later 134

8 *Mary:*
She was Always Attracted to the "Bad Boys".................................... 138

9 *Carol:*
Falling in Love With Someone Outside of Your
Marriage...What's Next? 145

CONCLUSION: TRAUMA TEACHES US WHAT LIFE IS ALL ABOUT

10 *Life is a Bitch and Then You Die:*
Growing, Evolving, and Discovering the Real
Meaning of Your Whole Life 159

About The Author 181

Introduction:
Lessons We Learn as Babies

"Hello. It's very nice to meet you. I'm Rich Scheinberg." I greet every new client with faith, confidence, optimism and a great sense of adventure. The journey we are about to embark on may be long and arduous, but I am always sure the work will be fruitful and deeply rewarding.

I have faith that the human spirit will always prevail. Every baby teaches me that lesson. We are born with lots of energy and love to share. Babies' eyes are wide open, full of life and filled with trust. They are born with the notion of being seamlessly connected to the world. After all, they have been literally connected since conception. The umbilical cord and human body nurtures all of their physical and emotional needs from day one.

When we come out into the light of day, we continue to expect nurturing and sustenance. That sense of connection is part of the essence of life itself. That notion is affirmed every hour of every day. Mom, Dad, and other family members hold us and feed us throughout the day. Our every need is anticipated and acted on. A mother looks into her baby's eyes and can tell if the baby is comfortable or not. If she senses any discomfort, she will immediately attempt to alleviate the discomfort. You need a hug? Some milk? A clean diaper? Your wish is Mom's command. This is the best part of being a baby. There is the affirmation that the world is a place of connectedness, instant gratification and unconditional love.

Daddy also takes part in this family love fest. He is usually excited and eager to accommodate his child's every need. However, he can sometimes feel that Mom's connectedness to their new child takes away some of the time and attention he shared with Mom and so he may also experience some jealousy.

A child's life experience begins. On occasion, he or she finds out that his needs are not always fulfilled right away. Sometimes there is a great delay. Sometimes it seems there is no gratification at all.

In the early years, a child gets satisfaction from being able to master many of his own needs each day: moving from here to there, asking for food or a drink, and climbing into your lap to share a great big hug. But sometimes he feels confined. No one seems to understand what he feels, and the love seems nowhere to be found.

He can be deeply disappointed and hurt—emotionally and physically—and another reality emerges: the world can feel very disconnected. A child may lose his sense of trust and feel his or her needs can't be met. Additionally, a child may feel misunderstood or that no one loves him unconditionally for who he is. That is a very scary feeling.

Let me share with you a very personal experience. In my late twenties, I took part in an intensive therapy experience that lasted from a Friday evening to a Sunday afternoon. The weekend consisted of many therapeutic exercises designed to move quickly beyond defenses to "core" issues—those early experiences whose trauma may affect us consciously or subconsciously for years.

One exercise was designed to help the participant recover experiences they had as an infant. In a calm, safe and peaceful setting, we were instructed to imagine ourselves much younger.

"Imagine yourself at five years old... then four years... then three..."

Minutes later, we were infants being held and comforted by Mommy, loved and fed by bottle or breast. It was a very good feeling, a familiar feeling. I recalled being held close to my mother's bosom, feeling very warm. I remembered the blouse she would often wear with the print and collar. I remembered the position she would assume on her bed with the door left slightly ajar. I remembered the bedroom in the old house down at the end of the hallway and to the right. In that bedroom, I lay in my mother's arms, sucking at her breast, getting nourishment. My fingers would always find their way up to her collar where I enjoyed manipulating the pointy end of the collar material between my thumb and fingers while I nursed, feeling love, comfort and safety.

"Now I want you to imagine that your bottle or breast is being pulled away from you," the therapist instructed. "You can no longer have it..."

I began to feel upset. The image of losing my mother's breast was clear in my mind.

"How do you feel now?" the therapist prompted.

I didn't like this feeling at all. I was tempted to detach myself from the visualization.

"Stay with the feeling," the therapist said, as if he knew what I was thinking. "See where it takes you."

I started to cry. I didn't exactly know why. I also heard others sobbing around the room.

"Crying is okay," the therapist assured us. "It's in you and it needs to come out. See where it takes you."

Out of pure faith, I faced my fear of losing control over my feelings. I continued to cry, like a baby in deep pain. Soon I found myself in my old, white crib. "Mommy, Mommy!" I called out silently.

"It's time to go to sleep," I could hear her call from downstairs.

I went to the corner of the crib and looked for her through the crack of the doorway. "Mommy, Mommy!" I called out again.

"Go to sleep," she told me.

It was a memory that represented a daily occurrence. It was a memory that culminated in the realization that, at a certain time of the night, she was never coming up to check on me.

"It's past your bedtime." I understood at twelve months. It meant I would be alone for the rest of the dark night. I felt very lonely just remembering it. I was very upset. I continued to cry.

Then I gradually curled up in the corner of that crib, pressed against the vertical white bars and cried myself to sleep.

When I opened my eyes at least forty-five minutes later, the room was half-empty. A female participant stayed to comfort me. My therapist was there too. Without words, this profound experience helped me to discover the source of my distrust of others. This was not the experience of just one incident. This was my first memory of my mother's turmoil and detachment, of my father's lack of involvement in child rearing, of the dysfunction in my family, mandating that each one must fend for him- or herself. Part of me held on to the faith that my mother still loved me. Part of me gave up the belief that I was ever loved at all.

Most of us, through our own sequence of experiences, have had to grapple with the core question of whether or not we are really lovable.

Furthermore, we might ask, are we born lovable or do we have to earn it by being or acting a certain way?

By age one, I believe that most of us have experienced this dual reality. We are filled with a sense of connection to everyone and feel unconditional love—love without limits. The other world is filled with conditional love, distrust, alienation and fear. And so the journey begins.

My clients are those who are keenly aware of this dual reality. They remember an earlier time when love was all around them. They may have seen love in action in other families. Or perhaps they saw a glimpse of it in a relative or friend, a character in a movie, or on Oprah. They know that real love, unconditional love, exists. Some may feel that it doesn't seem to exist for them right here, right now. People who enter therapy are smart, sensitive people searching for a simple birthright: to live with a minimum of fear and hurt. They want to reconstruct a life in which people listen to needs expressed verbally and nonverbally, in which people can be trusted to respond in a way that affirms their importance. It is a world in which you are connected and where you want to be loved without having to do anything to earn it. Just like a baby, you are loved just as you are, without condition or expectations.

My faith in therapy is that every person who seeks to reclaim this birthright will find it. My job is to help a client learn to trust again, to go after connections to others, and most of all, to accept and love him—or herself without condition. I tell my clients that they must appreciate their own unique qualities and talents before they can expect others to do the same. I tell them never to let other people's perceptions define them. Other people are dealing with their own fears and insecurities which always interfere with their ability to know and love others. I tell my clients, "Only you can know, appreciate, and love you best."

My confidence in the process of therapy comes from hundreds of individuals, couples and families I have worked with over the twenty-five years I have been in practice. I am fortunate enough to have been involved in countless situations where the human spirit has prevailed. Sometimes the work takes an hour, sometimes it takes a few weeks and sometimes it takes a few years. My experience is that, without exception, insight, relief and love come to all who seek it. The bigger the quest for the adventure called Life, the deeper the insight, the greater the number of lessons learned, and the most love of life is achieved.

I'm Crazy Enough to Think That There is a Solution to Every Problem

During the first half of my life, I was a lone wolf and a lost soul—and I was proud of it. I was married with many friends and a big family, but I was fiercely independent. I prided myself that I had spent many years overcoming a myriad of personal struggles without asking anyone for help.

I relied on my intellect to solve my problems. My emotions were always under control and I had no faith that any God or spirit was available to help me. Emotionally, I often felt alone in my struggles, but I felt quite capable of being able to survive any adversity.

My dysfunctional family history became my "School of Hard Knocks" and it was my original motivation for attaining a college degree in psychology. Navigating constant and chronic family conflict became "boot camp" for entering the field of human relations.

My bachelor's degree led me to gratifying work with children and adolescents who had been removed from their New York City family environments and placed in an institutional setting in upstate New York. These boys were angry and streetwise, but they were also needy for a young adult who could relate to their overwhelming sense of isolation and pain. I easily identified with these feelings. Though we all maintained our stoic male exteriors, we quickly developed an unspoken kinship and a connection that I will never forget.

When it came time to start graduate school, I realized that I had to move back to Long Island to enroll in a master's program in social work. The idea of separating from the adolescents was difficult, but I realized I had no choice if I wanted to pursue a career in the field.

I had gotten married while working in the group home. My wife, Gerry, and I realized that I would have to further my education if we were ever to afford having our own home and family.

Since I had a few years' experience in a group home and Gerry had helped as a houseparent, we decided to take a similar job on Long Island. This time we were required to supervise the daily activities of nine mentally retarded adults. The job offered a decent salary and fifty percent tuition reimbursement. It also offered free rent. The only catch was that we had to live in the same house as the people we were caring for. They were very nice people, but it often seemed like we were working twenty-four hours a day.

Originally, I had thought the job would be a great opportunity. In fact, it seemed to be the only way we could afford to live while I attended graduate school. But only a month after moving into our new home and working at the new job, I started to have serious regrets. At first I thought I just needed time to adjust. But I began to fill with resentment and doubt. My wife became concerned about me.

"Are you okay?" she asked one day.

"I'm fine," I insisted. After all, I thought I was the strong one in the relationship. I never allowed myself to need or depend on anyone my whole life, not even my new wife. I'd survived much worse, I thought.

But each morning brought more pain. The depression felt so heavy that I could feel it pervade every inch of my body. I finally decided to go to a medical doctor for a prescription. Medication had helped me get through one of my dark times once before and I thought once again it was time for some help with my adjustment.

After a brief interview, my doctor offered me anti-depressant medication. "I'm not depressed," I protested, still in denial. "I just need something to help me adjust. I think I need some Valium."

"Valium?" the doctor asked. "We usually prescribe Valium for anxiety, not depression."

"I'm sure Valium will help me," I insisted. "I took it once before when I lived away at college and it worked great."

"Okay, we'll try it then," replied the doctor. "Then you can let me know if you have any problem."

I went home feeling victorious. I thought only I knew what was best for me. But after several mornings, I realized the Valium was not helping. Fear began to set in. The emotional and physical pain was worse than ever. In addition, I started to have a strange feeling that I was becoming detached from the world. I began to feel a sense of numbness to life itself. My body was going through the daily activity of life, but the emotion or purpose was getting lost somewhere.

"Are you okay?" my wife asked repeatedly, more and more worried.

"I'm okay. I can handle it," was my ongoing response. But each morning, I was troubled by the mere light of day. My only hope was to keep busy all day so that nighttime would come more quickly and I could fall asleep again. Soon, I started to fantasize that I would never wake up.

I wondered whether I should quit the job and move out of the house. But that would mean admitting to a complete failure in judgment and decision-making. I decided I couldn't live with that shame. And then where would Gerry and I live with no income? Back with Mom and Dad? Since my teenage years, one of my main goals in life had been to achieve independence from my parents, who seemed strict and unreasonable. Asking them for help was not an option.

I continued to fantasize about finding peace. I categorically ruled out all options. Then I thought of one more possibility: going to a psychotherapist. Even though I could not, even in my deepest despair, confide in my wife, I felt safer consulting a professional who was outside of my family. In this way, I could protect my hard-earned reputation as a smart, self-reliant man.

Filled with doubt about how a stranger could offer me advice, I was determined to see whether there was a glimmer of hope that would convince me that I could find peace in this life.

As I entered the therapy room, I smelled incense. I guess this is still the Seventies, I joked silently to myself, but let's see if this guy can actually tell me anything about how to relax. This incense isn't doing it for me at all.

"Come right in," he said in his soft voice. "How can I help you?"

I proceeded to tell him my laundry list of complaints, daring him to come up with at least one real solution.

The therapist responded in the way I had anticipated: "Oh, I see you are having a lot of difficulty. We are going to have to explore that one a little further. Yes, we will have a lot to talk about in the weeks to come..."

I don't have weeks, I thought, and I was clever enough to avoid mentioning the thought of suicide at any time during the session. As I exited the room, I thought, I knew it. No one could ever come up with an idea I haven't already thought about. So, since the session didn't help, there was only one option left. I couldn't cope with the pain any longer.

I decided that my full prescription bottle of Valium would do it. I was careful not to mix any alcohol or any other drug into the plan since I had a weak stomach and I didn't want to take a chance that I would vomit it back up. I intended on doing this once and I was determined to do it right.

A few mornings later, I left the house, telling my wife that I was on my way to class. As usual, Gerry knew I had much more to say, but she did not try to press the issue. I drove to a remote, wooded area I had not seen before. I parked my car and walked into the woods for about twenty minutes, hoping to get lost. With a last act of self-reliance and conviction, I gulped down the whole bottle of Valium with a can of soda. Soon after that, I curled up into a fetal position at the base of a tree and fell asleep. I was determined to find peace at last.

Some time later, I recalled waking up, feeling disorientated and dizzy. Somehow I staggered from tree to tree and found my way out of the woods. Apparently, it was not my time to leave this world. I found my way back into my car and got it running. But I couldn't figure out how to make it go. Suddenly, a police officer appeared at the window and startled me.

"Are you drunk?" he yelled.

"No," I replied in all sincerity.

"Well, you're either going to jail or the hospital," the officer said.

Now that choice didn't require much thought.

"The hospital," I replied.

Upon interrogation, I admitted my attempt to take

my own life. After emptying my stomach, I was admitted to the locked psychiatric ward. Day after day, I attended daily activities with other patients, many of whom had severe mood disorders. One young woman would scream uncontrollably. An older woman was in residence to receive her third round of electroshock therapy. I was scared. My wife, father-in-law, and friend, Eileen, came to visit and offer much-needed support. But I didn't see my own mother, father or brothers and they didn't call either.

I had to get out of there. After a week, I made a deal with the attending psychiatrist: If he would allow me out of that asylum, I would not attempt suicide again and I would go to psychotherapy. I was actually serious about making another attempt, but I wanted to get out very badly. The psychiatrist agreed to release me from the hospital, but he wisely warned Gerry not to let me out of her sight.

Now out of the hospital, I kept my word and I began to see a new clinical social worker, "Carmine." Once again, I went through the motions of reporting my recent history with no desire or expectation of help.

Carmine looked at me intently. "Were you a good boy?" he asked.

What kind of stupid question is that? I thought. "Yeah, sure," I replied.

"Were you always good?" Carmine continued.

"Yes, I was," I replied. "I knew better. It was my brother Dale who didn't follow the rules. My father used to beat him almost every night."

"So what did you do with your anger?" Carmine probed.

"Me? I wasn't angry. My father was angry. I don't believe in getting angry. Anger is destructive. It only causes pain." I grew up in the '60s and I was a hippie at heart. Love was good. "Love is all you need," the Beatles sang. Anger was bad. I tried to exorcise it from my mind like it was poison.

"But if you were so good in such a sick family, then you must be very, very angry," Carmine insisted.

I paused, thought about it, then thought about it again. Carmine was right. I was very, very angry about the atmosphere in my family as I was growing up. I was angry at my mother. She was always depressed and preoccupied with her own needs. She said she loved me, but I never felt it. I felt abandoned instead.

I was angry at my father, too. He was preoccupied with working, "to put a roof over our heads," as he said. He complained about money, never trusting my mother with his money. He seemed always to be angry with her. I never heard the word "love" come out of his mouth. In fact, I rarely heard him utter a kind word to anyone in the family when I grew up... that is, unless we had company visiting. The only personal knowledge I had of him came from my mother, who feared and hated him. I was angry that I always had to keep a safe distance from him. I was always alienated and isolated in my family. To survive, I had to bury all of my emotions, yet inside I was angry enough to kill. Depressed and angry enough to kill myself!

"I guess you're right," I admitted. "I never thought about it that way before." I hesitated. "But what good can come out of being angry?"

"You have to allow yourself to feel and be whatever you are before you can address the issues and find some answers."

That made sense. It was the beginning of thinking about my life in a whole new way. It would be a long, hard struggle. I would have to give up being the strong, silent survivor. And I would have to start confiding in my wife and friends.

I started to realize that I wasn't alone after all. My therapist understood me. And when I started to open up, my wife understood me too. Apparently, the notion of being alone and feeling separate from everyone stemmed from a family pattern. I began to learn how to communicate and feel connected to the world. I started to develop a new and deeply spiritual awareness about life. I thought that my life had lost its meaning. I thought there was no hope left— nothing to live for. But I was dead wrong. It was not my time to go. On the contrary, facing death made me realize that I had nothing to lose by letting go of all my previous assumptions about life.

This trauma forced me to do the deepest soul-searching of my life. Over many, many months I painstakingly reviewed and resolved every source of conflict and despair in my life. And the payoff for this work has been greater than I could have ever imagined. The result of this trauma was a spiritual rebirth I could not deny. I came to realize that my life has a purpose that only a higher power could have understood. I know now that I am very much like every other individual who feels like a lost soul on this earth.

As I developed more faith and learned how to heal my pain, I realized that my life's purpose is to share my knowledge and insight. Furthermore, as I have learned, we always have a choice to ask those around us to help ease our burden, physically and spiritually. My experience and faith in this healing process has led me to greet each new client with a "crazy" sense of optimism. This is quite a contrast to each client's expectation.

"John" walks through my door looking beaten down by life and exhausted. His head is lowered, his eyes are looking downward, and his stomach is tight. He starts to look up to receive my greeting. I look into his eyes, the "windows of the soul." I see a light growing dim. I see the human spirit struggling to survive. I see fear, hurt, pain and anger. I understand these feelings. I know these feelings. I have had personal experiences with the vast range of human emotions. I instantly feel a connection. I reach out and shake the hand of my new client. I look at him deeply and verbalize a sincere "Nice to meet you."

I intuitively gather as much information as possible. I quickly and playfully test my mind-reading skills. I used to think that I was good at making educated guesses regarding a client's problem, but I have come to believe that there is also an emotional "frequency" that I can tune in to and sometimes information seems to just pop into my head. I imagine how he is feeling.

John senses that even though I'm a stranger to him, I seem to care. He sits down with a sense that he has met a new friend rather than an analyst. So far he does not feel judged, but he is full of anxious anticipation. As he starts to describe his predicament, he can't seem to get the words out fast enough. There is so much to say, so much damage done, so many incidents, failures in communication, failed relationships, broken dreams.

"Where do I begin?" he asks.

"It doesn't matter where you begin," I reply. "Just keep talking and I'll keep listening."

Like a sponge, I try to absorb all of the information while furiously taking notes on my clipboard. After about fifteen minutes, a picture starts to emerge.

I get an idea of how, when and where the hurt began. I get an idea how much damage has been done. I get an idea how much time it will take John to start to heal and start to feel some relief from his emotional pain.

After about twenty minutes, I tell him, "You've obviously been through a lot. Now I understand how all of this has accumulated to a point where you can't take it anymore." John has doubted that anyone can appreciate his pain, but I start taking the liberty to describe how he must feel toward his mother, father, and lover. I am able to give clarity and specific words to describe the barrage of emotions he expressed just moments earlier.

"It's amazing," he says. "You're able to describe how I feel better than I can. I like how you're able to find just the right words to use."

"I've had lots of practice finding the right words to describe how people feel," I explain. "It's important for you to know that a lot of people have had very similar feelings to yours at some point in their lives." John is glad to hear that he is not alone in his struggle. I look him right in the eyes. "You know, even I have had some of those feelings. I'm human too," I reassure him.

John sees in my eyes that I know how he feels. He doesn't need to know what I've been through. He only needs to know that I'm okay now and that I'm extremely confident that his hopeless problem is no mystery to me and that I know a resolution is well within reach.

The therapy hour goes quickly, but we are not finished until I give John complete reassurance that his hurt, alienation and pain can be relieved. John, in his desperation, dares to believe that for the first time in many years, he may be able to reconnect on a deep level with another human being. It is an old and welcome feeling. I describe a plan to address all of the problems he has just presented. I emphasize that I will not fix the problems. I am only a coach or facilitator to help him find his own answers to the dilemmas he has just described. We are a team that will work together toward the common goal of understanding and alleviating his fear, hurt, pain and anger.

John is gratified that I listen well and that I seem to have a good grasp of his predicament. He is also impressed that I am able to develop an "action plan" so quickly, since all seemed so hopeless just an hour earlier. But what really puzzles him is my confidence. How could I be so sure that I can help someone with a problem as bad as his?

What John doesn't know is that I believe that the human spirit and the spirit that transcends all life have instilled in me an undying optimism. My confidence is not so much based on faith as it is based on my personal history. He does not know that I meet each new client with the expectation of being able to relate personally to any problem that may be presented. "A little presumptuous," you say? "Maybe so," I reply.

After many years, I have come to realize that my own life challenges were actually blessings in disguise. The profound lessons I've learned have taught me that the purpose of my life has been to appreciate keenly the dual reality of life. The deep pain—the traumas—and cathartic realizations—the triumphs—are the contrasts that give life its meaning. After my own long, soul-searching journey from trauma to triumph, I now love life so much that I can't wait for each new day. I want to learn about and experience everything that life has to offer. With the help of my higher power, I have survived many years of hopelessness and desperation. My own experience dictates the optimism and confidence that I bring to every new client I meet. The affirmation and mantra I repeat silently to myself is "I made it through and so can you."

We All Have the Same Issues—More or Less

The pain of feeling alienated and misunderstood is the universal fear and anxiety that dims the spirit. The hurt usually involves an experience of trusting or seeking love, but experiencing betrayal and/or abuse. Sometimes the hurt is traumatic and sometimes the pain is so great that one has fantasies of homicide or suicide. Some experiences are more common in childhood and some occur more often in adulthood. As we look back, we always try to make sense of it all. "Why did this happen to me?" "What am I supposed to do now?" "Does God have a plan?" "Do I have a purpose?" These are experiences to which we can all relate.

Healing starts as soon as one feels connected and understood by at least one other person. Sometimes that person is a relative or friend. Sometimes that person is me. It is extremely important for you to know that your problem or fear is not unique. It is normal. It is to be expected. In fact, your problem is one that is shared by thousands, if not millions, of people. Life is not a noun. It's a verb. Life's most important experiences are not so memorable because of where you are, but where you have been—and what you learned in order to get where you are. When you meet someone new, you'll always find that the person's journey is much more interesting than that person's current life status.

Don't be fooled into thinking that "other people" have it easier than you do. Those that seem on the outside to have the fewest problems just happen to be the best actors. You just have to scratch the surface to know better.

Sure—some people have more problems than others. But the people who have dealt with more problems are much more interesting and they make the best friends. They tend to be better listeners, they are more empathic and insightful and they offer the best advice. When a person has survived the most difficult problems in life, I consider him (or her) as having graduated from the "Harvard School of Life," and I have the utmost compassion and respect for that person. These are the "old souls" who are my closest friends.

The connection of spirit established at the first individual session is multiplied by those who dare to enter group therapy. I always love to witness individuals discovering first hand that their shameful, secret problems are shared in one form or another by many others.

That is where I began to dream about writing this book. By sharing a sampling of the innermost conflicts of nine of my clients, as well as a sampling of my own personal experiences, you, the reader, may also find some relief for what you are burdened with right now. You are not alone. You are just like the rest of the human race. Also, it is important to have faith that the human spirit that brought you into this world is always with you even when you feel most alone. That spirit unites us all and is more powerful than you may realize.

In this book you will meet ten people, (including myself), who have moved from trauma to triumph.

You may recognize yourself in some of the stories. Or you may not. I hope that the journey these ten people have taken will serve as inspiration for you should you ever need to go from trauma to triumph in your own life.

Your Personal Connection to the Power of Spirit

My zest to harness the power of spirit in human form has been a labor of love and a work of art. My approach is generally considered traditional, eclectic psychotherapy with a strong emphasis on client-centered directions and goals. Each person decides whether therapy means getting through just the immediate crisis or whether more "core" problems need to be addressed.

The depth and length of therapy is purely a personal choice. I completely respect a client's choice to "process" his or her life experience in a few short hours, during several months or over the span of several years. When clients wish to explore every possible avenue to personal growth, I try to accommodate them as much as I can by offering them more creative, holistic and spiritually-evoking forms of psychotherapy.

My early background included training and experiences in Freudian therapy, behaviorism, and Rogerian client-centered therapy. Then I experienced

Transcendental Meditation and Psychodrama while still in undergraduate school. I entered my personal psychotherapy while still in graduate school and I experienced Transactional Analysis and Gestalt therapy. I was also involved in group therapy for many years.

Most recently, I have been fascinated by the "energy" therapies (Eye Movement Desensitization Reprocessing, Thought Field Therapy, Emotional Freedom Technique) and body-centered therapies. I became certified as a "Reiki" practitioner and "Reconnective Healing" practitioner to experience the warmth and vibration of healing energy in my hands. I have also been trained to use hypnosis for Past Life Regression therapy. It is another amazing technique for personal growth that I will address more specifically in another manuscript, to be completed shortly.

So this book is intended to facilitate the connection that unites all of us—in this lifetime and beyond. I have come to believe that problems are intended to open new doors and provide new insights. I believe that problems are actually blessings in disguise.

The stories you are about to read are very real. Only the details have been disguised to protect the identity and confidence of each brave soul who has chosen to embark on processing his or her personal journey. Each of them has been inspired and each one has expressed the desire that you will read this book and also be inspired.

The healing that you will witness will come as a result of each person's attempt to follow the love of spirit or the direction of the Higher Self. I believe the drive to claim a sense of connection and love in relationships is innate at birth. Again, I see my personal role as a "coach" or facilitator in this search for peace, insight and purpose to be instrumental— but secondary. Therefore, each story is intended to focus on the individual efforts rather than my own interventions. So please read this book and become a part of the conscious collaborative effort.

1
Yvonne:
Being a Child, Feeling Alone,
Then Learning to Trust

W e *all* have a very difficult time learning how to trust others. Here, Yvonne begins with her mom.

"Dear Mom,

I'm writing this letter today only because I'm in a good mood and perhaps feeling a little level headed and we all know I'm always a little more comfortable writing all my thoughts down rather flying off the handle at you and dad. Mind you, I will warn you now, this letter will be far from grammatically correct or in order. It's obvious that I am more than annoyed with you several times a week if not a day. I can't begin to start now after all this time bringing up things that I'm pissed about from years ago, but I'm gonna anyway. Not to be sooo dramatic, but the day grandpa passed away, everything changed. I don't know if it's when I changed or you changed or the whole family in general. But I associate his death with nothing but chaos. I, of course, loved grandpa with all my heart, but I'm just using that day to pin point the time. The only thing I can remember about high school is being by myself. I remember hating you and dad and your entire extended family. I remember hating my brother Tom... and I could never really get why. I don't exactly hate anyone these days, but I still get sooooo agitated to the point where I wanna cause some serious physical or emotional harm to all of you. Whether it be something I say or do/don't. I feel like my entire life I've been looked at like I can do anything by myself... and granted, it would be fucking wonderful if I could, but I'm only 21 and I do need help sometimes, but it's come to the point where I'm almost afraid to ever ask for help. Although if I do finally ask... I have to hear about it forever. I have to hear that the only reason I speak to you guys is when I need money and that's pretty much how it is now. Because I feel like I don't even wanna discuss anything with you. I don't want you to know anything about my life b/c you never bothered to care ...

We stopped being a family long before you and dad decided to separate or at least I feel like I wasn't a part of it. You and Dad hurt me soooo much and never once did you, not dad, act like you cared. You almost act like I deserved something like this b/c grandma did it to you.

You're not a bad person. You really aren't, but

sometimes the things I hate most about what happened just consume me... and I can't stop thinking about it. I just can't get over it. I still get aggravated with the drinking... You don't know how much I hate it. And I don't think that will ever change. When I see it... I just get all these flashbacks that I can't stop thinking about. I think this is the purpose of this letter. I don't want to resent you anymore. I just want you to be my mom.... I love you mom. I really do, with all my heart."

Yvonne was a very pretty young woman with dark brown hair and blue eyes who carried her problems as excess weight on her small-framed, five-foot-tall body. When I looked at her, I felt sadness. But when I looked a little deeper, I also saw a spark of life and vitality that was determined to keep her alive. I was confident that she could succeed.

When I began seeing Yvonne, she was a troubled young woman who hated her parents—her mother more than her father. Her parents both drank heavily. She also had a younger brother, Tom, who seemed to get all of her parents' attention.

Many years before, I had counseled Yvonne's parents. They were nice people, but they didn't expect much from each other. The drinking habits got better for a while and then they got worse. Their sessions had focused on their marital turmoil; the spirit that had once united them seemed long lost. They also mentioned their younger child, Tom, who seemed to be having problems as well. Yvonne was their older daughter who was always described as a child who "could take care of herself." Her name was rarely mentioned.

Yvonne's parents eventually gave up on each other: They dropped out of therapy and two years later, they got divorced. Her mother realized that the breakup affected their daughter more than their son. She started to worry that Yvonne, now twenty-one, was starting to get depressed. That's when she called me to ask if I would start working with her daughter.

Yvonne spent our first session venting about all the things that were bothering her. In my office, she seemed much more angry than depressed. She seemed to enjoy having a place to finally vent her frustrations and pain. She told me how she hated both of her parents but at the same time, she reminisced about having had a much better relationship with her mother when she was younger.

After weeks and weeks of going over Yvonne's issues with her, one thing kept coming up—hatred for her mother. She had good early memories of her mother, but now the relationship was far from good. I talked to Yvonne about confronting her mother about all this anger. She said that she couldn't. I suggested that we could have a session with her mother and go over Yvonne's feelings, but she didn't feel that she could do that either. I then talked to her about writing a letter to her mother. She didn't have to give it to her, but she needed to get all those feelings out. They were consuming her. She needed to get it all off her chest. So Yvonne decided to write that letter, which is the one that began this chapter.

The letter was a great expression, a purging, of all her emotions regarding her mother. It was raw and honest. It revealed very negative emotions that had been harbored all of these years. It exposed an overview of hurt, anger and alienation. Yvonne handed me this letter with great trepidation. In her mind, this letter would show me how "ugly" she could be.

As I read the letter, I knew that Yvonne had "opened a door" and invited me into a very private place that was unknown to the rest of the world. This letter was an abstract of her emotional diary: raw, uncensored feelings that she wished to share with someone else, but would never dare. Inner conflict immediately arises from the need to trust someone with these tender feelings—but shame and fear of betrayal preclude this option.

As I read of this young woman's heartache, another part of me silently recalled writing about similar hurt in my own personal diary many years ago. I finished the letter and looked up at Yvonne. Her eyes were filled with tears and apprehension.

"I love it!" I exclaimed. "It's very raw and very beautiful."

Yvonne was puzzled—no, she was shocked that I

had said that. She felt like it was a horrible letter to write to one's own mother. (She didn't give it to her mother.) I told her that it was a gift. Sure, it was about loads of anger and even hatred for her mother, but it was also a great expression of wanting to reconnect with her as well. She still had a lot of love for her mother. In fact, that love was the reason behind the letter. Yvonne wanted a relationship with her mother. She started to see what I meant about it being a gift. Since she saw me as sort of a father figure, it really meant a lot to her that I, as a parent myself, could see this as a good thing. Even though Yvonne didn't give her mother the letter, on many levels it was a gratifying and sobering experience.

As Yvonne externalized her anger within the safe walls of my office, she was able to cope with more of the pressure that was overwhelming her and causing her to shut down outside in the real world. This depression had often caused Yvonne to wake up late for her college classes. Sometimes, she would not go at all. In fact, Yvonne was forced to withdraw from all of her courses one semester to avoid failing grades.

Yvonne's depression and pain had also led her to her own drinking problem. She and her friends had a weekly ritual of going out "clubbing" every Friday night. Yvonne had the reputation of being able to drink the most and laugh the loudest. She attracted a lot of attention, but she also needed a few hugs.

The guys who took her home were a lot of fun, at least as much as she could remember. Then they would leave late at night or first thing in the morning. They always took her number, but they would never call again. Sometimes Yvonne would see one of them at the club weeks later. Glances were exchanged, but not a word was spoken.

Yvonne didn't trust anyone anymore—at least, not until I read her letter. That was the first time in years that she had revealed a deeply concealed emotion and someone had acknowledged the value of that emotion. It reminded her of the open, happy relationship she had often enjoyed with her mother as a younger child. Now we had a chance to talk about the issue of trust and how to rebuild it in all of her relationships.

"It really starts with you," I declared.

"No, it's other people I can't trust," Yvonne challenged.

"First, you have to trust your own gut feelings— meaning that the emotions you feel deep inside need to make sense to you."

"But I'm very confused about what I feel," responded Yvonne. "That's why I'm here talking to you," she added with a little sarcasm.

"Yes, that's the process of therapy," I explained. "I want to hear about everything you've been feeling deep inside all of these past years. I will listen very closely and together we'll sort out how your feelings make sense."

"What?" Yvonne asked with a smirk.

"Based on everything you've been through, everything you feel makes sense."

"How can you be so sure when I'm not sure myself?" Yvonne persisted.

"Let's use your letter to your mother as an example. On the surface, it may seem to be a confused mess of love, hate and anger toward the same woman at the same time."

"Yes."

"At first, that may seem to be contradictory. But now that we are having a chance to go over your feelings each week in detail, it makes complete sense for you to have had all of these feelings at one time or another... or even all three at the very same time."

"That's true. Now I understand and I don't feel like a crazy spoiled brat," Yvonne added with a deep sigh.

"So now you know why you feel the way you feel and now you can trust the way you feel," I said, with reassurance.

"Now I know I'm sane," Yvonne declared. "It's everyone else that's crazy."

"Not exactly," I said. "Trust starts with getting to know yourself and trusting your own feelings. When you feel more confident in your own skin, you naturally feel more daring about being yourself and being more open with others."

"Yes," Yvonne prompted, wondering where this

was leading.

"This is when you start finding out who you can trust. When you are able to show other people the "real" you, observe how they respond. Do they accept who you are? Do they care about what you say or do? Do they continue to like you when they disagree with you? Then maybe you can trust them."

"But what if they think I'm a jerk?"

"If they are so quick to criticize you without trying to understand you, then they are not trustworthy."

"Then what do I do?" Yvonne asked.

"First you need to understand that this is their problem, not yours. If they are so quick to judge others, then they may not have what it takes to be a good friend - not to you or anyone else. The only thing you can do is realize that you cannot trust this person at this time regarding this issue. This person may be treated like more of an acquaintance than a close friend."

"But what if everyone has something bad to say?" Yvonne worried.

"I'm sure that once you try this out, you'll be pleasantly surprised," I said with confidence. "Even if it turns out that less than half of your family and friends can be trusted to like or love you unconditionally, that's still a lot of people. And the chosen few can become your little support system for a long time to come."

"I hope you're right," responded Yvonne.

"I'm sure more people love you and want to be close friends with you than you realize," I reassured her with a smile.

In the months that followed, Yvonne continued to sort out most of her feelings. She often focused specifically on her mother and her father, hoping to recover some sense of trust in her relationship with each of them. Then she arrived at a great revelation. Most of the time, her parents' inability to respond to her needs actually had nothing to do with her. In fact, their behavior at home was more of a reflection of their own confusion and their own unmet needs.

Gradually, she was able to see that her parents had not purposely neglected her. It seemed that they were "still twenty-one years old" inside as well, and they had just gotten "lost" somewhere along the way. Little by little, she let go of feeling victimized and she became much more compassionate toward her parents.

In the weeks to come, Yvonne surprised herself that she didn't need to create a big scene and confront her mother. She gained an understanding of her mother even without talking to her. She started to feel more forgiving rather than angry and this new feeling felt much better. Yvonne's tone with her mother changed. Her mother was surprised by her daughter's change in behavior even though she didn't verbalize it and she responded in kind. She was less angry and defensive with Yvonne and Mom related to her with more compassion as well.

This whole experience helped Yvonne rediscover a sense of trust. For the first time, she poured out her heart and found unconditional love and acceptance. She found this in the therapy room and the beginnings of the same with her mother. She was able to recognize, for the first time in years, the part of her mother that wanted a healthy relationship. This was very gratifying. She could show her mother a way to recreate the relationship. As she let go of this negative baggage, she also found it easier to let go of her extra weight. She no longer needed to "stuff" down her discontent with food.

Yvonne was also proud of herself that she could piece this all together... and fairly quickly at that. As a result, her self-esteem and self-respect increased. The ability to understand and communicate these feelings spilled over to her relationships with men. She took more chances with speaking from her heart and was gratified with the response. This ability to trust men was news to Yvonne and she started to see it as a foundation for the beginning of her new life.

Currently, Yvonne has established many good relationships with people. She went from having lots of acquaintances and drinking buddies to having several close friendships. She went from having a long list of complaints and being negative about everything and everyone to feeling that she has the answers.

2

Carol:
Growing Up Being the Perfect Child
and Discovering Your True Self
as a Wife and Mother

Carol had been in therapy in another form when she came to me. However, she mentioned to a friend that she was feeling increasingly scared and that she had thoughts of "ending it all," she told me. That is when her friend became very alarmed and begged Carol to make an appointment with me. When Carol first walked into my office, she was dizzy with pain. I could see that pain in her eyes. I could tell that her head was spinning with all that was consuming her. She looked exhausted and her shoulders were hunched over as if she had the weight of the world bearing down on them. She seemed lost and confused. In her words, Carol needed "fast healing." She felt horrible and needed something immediately.

I started the session by asking her what she had gone over with others up to this point because I didn't want to repeat her therapy from scratch. She started to describe her previous therapy in vague terms.

"Olivia" would ask her a lot of questions, but she had been unable to find many answers. At first the questions felt caring, but soon Carol began to feel challenged and invalidated. She would often leave Olivia's office feeling worse than when she had arrived. Her stomach began to ache so much that she once vomited after her session. Curiously, Carol apologized about describing her previous therapist in such a negative way. Quickly, it became very clear that Carol was so "lost" about whom or what to trust that she could not even trust her own thoughts, opinions or experience.

This young woman was desperate for some emotional relief as soon as possible. And because she was so concerned about not overwhelming me with her problems, she came to the session prepared with a personal statement: a neatly typed summary of her life, "so you won't have to bother asking a lot," as she told me.

Half-jokingly, I stated, "You won't overwhelm me. I can handle it. In fact, if I spent as many hours as you trying to defend my feelings, I'd probably feel the same way."

As Carol handed me the letter, she blurted out, "So I'm not going crazy?"

I took the letter, replying: "So far, you're making complete sense to me." Then out of curiosity, I added, "Do you mind if I read it quickly right now?"

"No. Please do."

The letter read:

"My name is Carol Adams, I live in Freeport, New York and I'm 25 years old. I'm a full-time mom of three young girls and a part-time LPN. I work in a hospital with many gifted medical professionals. My goal is to reestablish my education by getting my undergraduate degree and then pursue my certification as a Physician's Assistant and join the ranks of these licensed, successful professionals.

I graduated from Uniondale High School in June of 1996 and attended Nassau Community College for nursing for approximately two years. After graduation, I worked for Long Island Jewish Medical Center as an LPN. It was a very fulfilling job, but this came to a close upon the birth of my first little blessing, a daughter in the fall of 1999. I then took a position at Mercy Hospital and worked all throughout the birth of my second little blessing, a daughter in 2001.

Life's excursion along the way had not been an easy one for my family. We had been dealt many difficult blows during this time. A husband who is a recovering alcoholic, a daughter who has Downs Syndrome and tremendous financial burdens. We owned a bar for a couple of years. Sadly, it robbed us not only of our blood, sweat and tears, but our money as well. During this time, I worked full time for three years while raising my daughters, I supported my husband, but somehow or other, got myself lost along the way. My third daughter wasn't planned, but she became my third blessing in 2003.

I've been with Mercy for about four years now. I am very happy and privileged to be working with people whom are not only in my eyes brilliant doctors and nurses, but with people I believe to be my second family. I've been told by my husband that he couldn't have asked for a more supportive wife—to him. I've been told by my friends that I'm a great mom. These are precious compliments, but what's equally uplifting is being told by co-workers and patients that I should go back to school because I'd be a great PA. I'm thinking they're right, it's my turn—to do for me."

Carol's letter read like a resumé. It told the facts of her life but did not tell about her feelings. She was not used to acknowledging her feelings, let alone talking about them, or putting her needs first. Only at the very end of her summary did Carol write about doing something for herself. She knew that she was lost and didn't have an identity. The only area where she felt things were going right for her was in her nursing career and plans for going back to school. But she still needed to find herself.

Carol's previous therapist told her that she had a "chemical imbalance" and "major depression" and needed to be put on the anti-depressant drug, Paxil. Carol said that she felt relief with the diagnosis. She felt like she had an answer to what was wrong with her, but I did not see it that way. I told her that I thought that she might want to hold off on taking medication for her symptoms and that maybe there were other reasons for her feeling depressed and confused. In my mind, I could tell that she was very depressed. But being challenged and invalidated is depressing. It's an understandable reaction, not a chemical imbalance.

However, Carol needed to get some relief from her depression by the end of that day. So I offered her another outlet. After reading her "resume" and discussing some of its content, I commented that she must be feeling very angry. Initially, she responded with a look of bewilderment. She had never thought of herself as angry. "Angry" always described "bad" people, and Carol always prided herself as being a "good girl," "good friend" and later, "good wife and mother." I went on to explain that in her case, her depression was caused by a tremendous amount of anger and frustration turned inward. Carol was a sensitive and passionate woman who had strong feelings and opinions about many things, but some of the issues might have caused an argument with her husband. And since "Carl" was a recovering alcoholic (and Carol was an understanding and supportive wife), she was not about to endanger his sobriety by confronting him with any controversial topics.

As a child, Carol was used to being a good girl by

not bothering the adults and going outside to play. She was careful not to annoy her father as soon as he came home from work, since Dad needed some quiet time before even Mom could talk to him about what was going on with the family each day. So as an adult, Carol knew how important it was not to let Carl get "wound up" about something.

Their daughters also had endless needs and it was important to Carol that she be the best mother she could be. She was always very patient and nurturing. Her children's happiness was the most important concern of her life.

What about Carol's needs and feelings? They came last. They accumulated inside and her pent up frustration was ready to burst out. This was her anger and now it was her turn to be heard.

So "feeling very angry" suddenly made sense and venting her frustration felt very, very good. Immediately, Carol had a look of relief and understanding on her face. Her body also loosened up and she was finally able to sit back in a comfortable position. She finally had a definition of what she was feeling and she knew that it was okay for her to have these feelings. Carol said that for the first time she felt a little bit of that weight come off her shoulders. She felt that her feelings had finally been validated. The therapy room became a safe and reliable forty-five minutes per week to let out years of pent up feelings and inner secrets.

A short time passed before Carol began to find consistent relief from her overwhelming feelings of depression without medication. She was able to accomplish this by using her anger as a guide to finding a long pattern of suppressed needs. Her pain and hurt had caused her to withdraw from "connecting" to others a long time ago. As a young child, her "secret" emotions had caused her to experience alienation and confusion. But ironically, she had learned to act like a very "good" girl on the outside. Acting like you are happy is exhausting. And very depressing. And it can't last long. Real feelings always need to surface. They have to surface somehow, in some way. So I always advise clients to choose which way they want to reveal themselves before some "emotional outburst" makes a statement in an unpredictable, "with-regrets" kind of way.

For Carol, being able to "connect" with me, expressing and venting all of her emotions, felt like a "slave being set free." I was careful not to judge or second-guess anything that she had to say. But Carol had more "demons" that she had kept secret.

After a few months, she was still of the opinion that there are always some feelings that are bad. There are some feelings that are destructive and better left unsaid. "There are some feelings I still get depressed about," she confided.

Was there any deep feeling that she would not risk revealing to me? Was there anything she would tell me that would change my opinion of her? "Yes, I think you would change your opinion of me," she replied. "Sometimes, I just feel the wrong thing," she added.

I asked her to tell me more. Facetiously, I prodded, "Have you killed anyone lately?"

Her laughter broke some of the tension. "No, that's not it," she replied.

"Well then, I can't think of anything you could tell me that would be so terrible or shocking," I added.

Carol decided to test my unconditional acceptance of her feelings. "I feel like I'm falling in love with a guy at work. He's a very nice guy. We've been talking a lot... it's not like I ever would cheat on my husband... but I can't stop thinking about this guy."

"How long do you know him?" I asked.

"For about six months," Carol replied. "We started talking at work and then we started having lunch together. We talk about everything. I tell him about Carl and the kids. And he tells me about his wife and kids. Lunchtime goes very fast... I feel like we could keep talking for hours."

"Well, that makes a lot of sense," I proclaimed.

Carol was puzzled. "What do you mean?"

"Here's a guy you can talk to about almost anything for hours—and you have so much to say. Why wouldn't you find that to be an attractive situation?"

"But then what?" she wondered. "What's next?"

"It's a dangerous situation," I agreed. "But before you start jumping to conclusions, let's go over this very carefully. This is a very difficult situation, but it is also rather predictable, given your situation. We'll go over your relationship with Bill piece by piece and the significance of the situation will become much clearer. Then you'll be able to figure out what comes next."

So the secret was out. Carol was getting involved in an affair that she couldn't discuss with anyone. This was the latest feeling to confuse her and it added another layer to her sense of shame and depression. But the very act of unburdening this information provided her with some relief. Hope replaced fear and shame. We would have more work to do together to sort this out. (Please see our exploration of Carol's "other" issue in Chapter Nine: Falling in Love with Someone Outside of Your Marriage... What's Next?)

3
Therese:
Growing Up with Sexual Abuse, Then Learning to Enjoy Sex and Forgive Your Past

Therese had been married a short time when her memories began to resurface. While taking a shower with her husband, she suddenly recovered an image of being a young girl in the shower with her father.

Therese complained to me that it was a disturbing memory that she had tried to forget, but couldn't. But I told her that it was too important to forget. It would affect her whether or not she could consciously remember it. So it would be to her advantage to try to remember as many of the details as possible, so that we could externalize the pain and attempt to do something about it.

Therese remembered being about five or six years old at a time when her father was unemployed and her mother worked during the day. She had spent the day with her father at the beach. When they returned home, Therese recalled getting undressed and into the shower to wash off the sand. She also remembered her father getting into the shower with her. Then her memory lapsed. The next event she remembered was her mother walking in with a look of shock and dismay on her face.

"What are you doing?" her mother exclaimed.

"We had to wash the sand off," replied her father.

Therese quickly ran out of the room, feeling fearful and ashamed. She preferred not to hear any more of the screaming that came from the bathroom. At this point, she apologized, telling me that she had felt something bad had happened in that bathroom, but she could not recall anything more specific. In fact, she wasn't sure whether any of it had really happened at all. She asked me whether she should try hypnosis to help her recover all of the possible details.

"No, I wouldn't suggest that right now," I replied, "unless it's something that you really want to do. The most important detail is that you felt you were sexually abused."

Whenever I speak to a child or adult about a memory of sexual abuse, my initial concern is about the emotional impression that is left. Later on, it may be important to recall the events and "evidence", particularly if legal recourse will be pursued, but for now, I was most concerned that Therese felt violated and "dirty." It was a feeling that had resurfaced years later while trying to take an intimate shower with her husband. It was a feeling that she didn't have the courage to even think about, let alone talk about, until she was much older. If I didn't care to hear more details to "corroborate" the veracity of this experience, how could I be so sure any of this actually happened? By looking for more evidence of emotional scars:

"Do you have any other early memories that may be sketchy, but difficult to talk about?" I asked.

"Yes," Therese admitted. "I remember that around the same time, I used to be very itchy... You know... down there."

"Your vagina?" I asked.

"Yes," replied Therese, her head lowered.

"Did you tell anybody about the itching?"

"Oh no," she exclaimed. "I felt 'dirty' talking about that area. I was afraid to tell anyone about it... I used to scratch a lot down there. Sometimes I scratched until it bled."

"And then what?" I prompted.

"I don't know... eventually, it just went away," Therese replied.

Therese also has an early memory of riding in the car with her father. He approached a particular house and noticed a red car in the driveway. Then he circled the block over and over again until the red car was gone.

"Then we parked around the corner from the house and walked to the side door where a woman let us in. After a short introduction, my father told me to go play in one of the rooms with my toys and not to bother them. Then the woman went into one of the bedrooms with my father and closed and locked the door. I had to play by myself for a long time, but I knew not to bother my father... It wasn't until I got older that I realized what they were doing."

Therese reported another traumatic memory at age ten when she started to develop into a young woman. Her aunt had given Therese her first bra and panty set, which she had preciously saved in her closet. Her father hated the gift because he had always (for some reason) hated the aunt who had purchased it. But Therese had treasured the gift anyway and she was waiting for some special occasion to wear it.

One evening, while she was playing in her room and her father and older brother were busy downstairs, Therese decided that she wanted to try on her new bra and panties. In the privacy of her room, she retrieved the set from her closet and tried it on. Therese admired herself in her dresser mirror, noticing her growing bosom and curvy hips. After several minutes, she reached back into her closet for another item, but in the process, she lost her balance. She fell to the floor and screamed, which brought her father and brother quickly up to the bedroom.

"What are you doing?" her father yelled.

"Just trying something on," Therese responded, apologetically.

"You have no business playing 'dress-up' now," her father retorted—and suddenly, he ripped her panties right off of her body.

"I just stood there in shock, crying," Therese explained, "and then I rushed to cover myself up. I couldn't believe my father would humiliate me so much—particularly right in front of my brother."

From that point on, Therese was careful to cover herself up at home. Though she became increasingly shapely, she made a point of wearing loose-fitting blouses and slacks. When she reached her teens and started to bring friends to the house, her father was inappropriate to her friends, also.

"He would leer at them and comment to them about looking sexy, which would embarrass me. He would also tell my friends how sexy I looked, adding 'I think she should pose for Playboy some day.' That was it. I realized that I could no longer have my friends come over to my house. It was too embarrassing."

Sexuality was something to fear and to hide. But at the same time, Therese was also learning something else about sex: There were times when a curvy body could have great power. And her teenage hormones reminded Therese that a "secret" pleasure could be obtained from "that area."

Therese had a difficult time with these heavily

conflicted sexual feelings throughout her adolescence. Her father also continued to reinforce the confusion. He spoke very crudely about women both in and out of the house, often commenting to her about passersby who had big breasts or whom he may "have a chance with." On the other hand, her father warned her not to be a "slut" like some other women and that if she ever wanted to "get a man," she had to remember that "a man doesn't buy a cow if he can get the milk for free." So Therese promised herself that she would remain a virgin until she got married.

"Harry" was a nice guy who was appalled by the way Therese's father treated her. He was older and established, and he was quickly able to see her as "his little butterfly with broken wings," as he liked to refer to her. Harry was able to gain her trust and she was able to overcome her fear of intimacy. Harry's love helped Therese come out of her "cocoon" and "spread her wings." After several months, the couple was engaged and they married a year later. Harry was glad that he had helped Therese "escape" her dysfunctional family and they planned to "start fresh" with a family of their own.

Therese was very grateful to her husband and her deep love allowed her to open up both emotionally and sexually in their relationship. As it turned out, she became a very passionate bride. A year after her marriage, Therese loved Harry deeply and she loved the romance that had developed between them. In fact, she began to plan many different Friday nights to celebrate their love.

Therese began to love her shapely body and she became more courageous about wearing sexy underwear and nightgowns with plunging necklines. On "special nights," she would become excited "dressing up" for Harry. Then she would fix her hair and make-up "just right." Lastly, she would fill the house with "mood music" and light several scented candles. She would not be able to wait until Harry came home from work so that she could surprise him as he walked in the door.

At first, Harry was wonderfully surprised and pleased. But as his wife took more and more of the initiative with their lovemaking, Harry became more and more uncomfortable. Therese didn't think much of it at first, but after several evenings that did not go as well as she had planned, she finally confronted Harry.

"What's the matter?"

"Nothing... I'm just tired tonight," he replied.

"No. It's got to be something else," she insisted. "This is the third time lately that we've had a problem."

"Well...when you get all dressed up like that and get so aggressive... you kind of act like a slut," Harry blurted out.

Therese was crushed. Again, the double message

came right back into her mind and pierced her trust and compassion like a dagger. Her heart raced and her thoughts became all scrambled.

"I didn't know what to think," she exclaimed. "At first I thought he was crazy. But then I started questioning myself. Was there something wrong with me? Was I really like a slut?" Therese didn't know, but she started feeling very scared. She then awkwardly threw on her robe and told Harry she was okay and just needed to relax by going downstairs and watching TV for awhile.

Harry let her go. He realized that he blurted out something very damaging, but he justified it in his own mind by thinking "She's getting a little carried away lately." Therese retreating downstairs allowed Harry to hold on to his position and he was somewhat relieved that he wasn't called on to defend himself. Harry was very uncomfortable that "his butterfly" had "spread her wings." For the moment, it wasn't clear if he could maintain the upper hand in the relationship.

In the days that followed, Therese would have second thoughts about taking the initiative in their relationship in a variety of circumstances. She felt disillusioned and even somewhat depressed. The "honeymoon" was over.

But it was safer not to talk about that night. Harry and Therese continued to talk about other things and they continued to hold hands, kiss and have sex, but the lovemaking wasn't as frequent or as exciting. Then they took a shower together...

It was another six months before Therese reached my office. Harry actually came with her that first evening and it was Harry who did most of the talking.

"She's tired all the time... She never comes to bed with me anymore. She just stays up late and then she sleeps late. Sometimes when I get home from work, she is still not dressed. And sometimes she hasn't even started dinner yet."

Then I turned to Therese. Her eyes were lowered and her spirit was dim. Her clothing was loose and wrinkled. I had this image of her shrinking into her clothes and disappearing completely into my couch. "Are you okay?" I asked gently, looking to cast a life jacket to her. "Do you want to tell me something about yourself?" I continued. Therese declined the invitation and then looked over at Harry.

Harry took the cue and he continued. "She grew up in a screwed-up family. Her mother worked a lot and she was never home. Her father was very abusive and she was always afraid of him. And I don't know what is the problem with her brother." Harry chose to be Therese's mouthpiece for most of the session. And she was all too willing to remain quiet and powerless. It was clear that Therese needed to be seen alone if she was going to be able to find her own voice.

During the second session, Therese confirmed all of the allegations that Harry had made about her father. The "shower scene" had brought it all back very graphically. During the next several months, as described earlier, we worked hard to recall and untangle all of her memories of abuse and betrayal.

While working on sorting out Therese's early memories, it became painfully evident that her shame and vulnerability became a source of "attraction" for Harry, an older man who preferred not to examine his own insecurities. Harry preferred to focus their conversations on "her crazy family" partly in order to avoid dysfunctional aspects of their own relationship.

The imbalance of power between Therese and her family and between Therese and Harry was eerily similar. In my office, Therese sought and expected me to be what most people think is the "traditional" therapist: I would listen to her problems and then I would give her lots of advice about how she should "fix" each problem. But that would reinforce the notion that her strength resided outside of herself.

Therese's best advice came from her inner voice—the voice that had been silenced a long time ago. I was determined to help this woman find her own personal power. Even when Therese habitually asked, "What am I supposed to say? What am I supposed to do?" I replied, "What do you want to say? What do you want to do? What would you say if you weren't worried about the consequences? What would you do if you had no fear?"

Therese found her answers inside. Her higher self or spirit spoke loud and clear, first in my office, and later "out in the real world." Over several months, she spoke up about years of victimization. Our sessions covered her early years, as well as her recent struggles with her husband.

As far as Harry was concerned, Therese was supposed to be just discussing her father with me. But when it became evident that his treatment of Therese was being discussed as well, Harry began to suggest to his wife that psychotherapy may not be the best way to address her problems. When Therese insisted that therapy was really helping her out of depression, Harry soon began to suggest that therapy was too expensive to continue. Then Therese felt well enough to get her own job and pay for her own therapy. She could no longer be silenced.

Her spirit and determination forced a change in her relationship with Harry. Her husband came to realize that if he didn't start taking her feelings and needs more seriously, their relationship would be irreparably damaged. Therese tried to impress Harry that she wasn't trying to get him to give her control over their relationship. After all, each person needed to maintain their own sense of power and freedom of choice. All that she was trying to get from Harry was for him to love her with all of her wants and needs intact. As Therese began to accept and love herself without humiliation or shame, she wanted Harry to be able to give her that same unconditional love.

The intensity of the marital struggle is beyond the scope of this chapter. However, it is important to note that Therese's hard work initiating the healthy repair of her marriage prepared her for an even greater challenge: repairing the relationship with her father.

Over the span of two years, Therese was able to rise out of her depression, return to work and pursue a successful career and take the initiative toward establishing a healthier marital relationship. But all of her success was tempered by the rediscovered awareness of the damage done to that "little girl" deep inside. Therese was living a "double" life. Part of her felt very strong and empowered. But the "inner child" still lived inside and in fear. Therese was now able to speak up to everyone around her, both at home and at work—but when her father called the house, she still hated to pick up the phone.

Mr. M. didn't know that Therese had worked through serious marital problems. He didn't know that his daughter had stopped taking her anti-depressant medication. Therese never even told him that she had sought psychotherapy two years earlier, because Mr. M. never believed in "airing your dirty laundry." Mr. M. only thought of Therese as "his little girl" who needed his guidance and advice. I asked Therese why she continued to become quiet and compliant each time her father called.

"Because if I start speaking up to him, he'll go into a rage," she replied. "He's too old to change now... It's easier just to let him talk, 'yes' him to death and then do what you want to do after you hang up the phone."

"So you don't mind spending twenty minutes on the phone or all day in person acting like a "good girl" for him?" I prodded.

"Well, I really hate it. But if I'm not nice to him, he'll never talk to me again," she insisted.

"So it's either take his criticism and sometimes even more verbal abuse or he will not talk to you again?"

"Yes, I guess so."

"Then what have you got to lose?"

Therese paused for a few moments. "Hmm, I guess you have a point there."

"Exactly. In fact, I think your father has a lot more to lose than you do. Your father is an angry, lonely man. He's a 'lost soul' with no place to turn. I believe he really loves you, but because of whatever background he endured, he has never known how to love anyone."

"Yes. He always told me some weird stories about Grandma and his family."

"So I don't think he'll be so ready to give up his relationship with you. If he loves you, he'll suffer much more of a loss than you would now."

"Yes, I can see that. He and Mom don't get along well. He hasn't spoken to my brother in months. And he doesn't have many friends left."

Over the next year, the phone calls took a different direction. When Therese didn't like something her father said, she started to interrupt his "lectures" and interject some of her own opinions. As predicted, Mr. M. would become offended and enraged. Sometimes he would start to scream and ask, "What's the matter with you lately?" Sometimes he called her "disrespectful" and "an ungrateful bitch," but Therese, with emotional support, was able to overcome her fear and cut the "conversation short."

After an altercation, the phone calls stopped for a week. Then a few weeks. Then two months. Therese started to panic.

"How do you feel about the situation?"

"Part of me is worried that he'll never talk to me again. And the other part of me is relieved that he'll never talk to me again."

Six months passed.

One day, Therese picked up the phone to hear her father's voice.

"I don't know what happened," he said, his voice choked up, "but I can't stand this anymore; I haven't seen or talked to you for a long time." Now he was ready to listen.

"I miss you too," replied Therese. "It's just that I

can't stand arguing with you anymore. I don't expect you to agree with a lot of what I have to say, but you can't talk down to me anymore. I'm a young woman now. I want you to talk to me like an adult. I need you to understand that I have opinions and feelings. I want you to think about that before you react to what I have to say."

"Okay, Therese," her father replied.

"Okay, Dad," said Therese.

That conservation was the start of Therese redefining their relationship. Over the next several months, many more talks would follow, both on the phone and in person. Mr. M. became more careful about the way he spoke to his daughter, but he needed to be reminded to "relax, Dad" by Therese when he started to raise his voice. Mr. M. was particularly difficult to confront in person. In the process of reviewing their relationship, Therese made an effort to visit her parents more often. Sometimes her mother, who had been recently diagnosed with ovarian cancer, was too sick to leave the house, so she would "be a good daughter" and volunteer to take her father out to do errands and go food shopping. These father/daughter trips seemed harmless at first, but Therese knew that she always needed to be emotionally prepared.

"Therese, look at the rack on that woman," exclaimed Mr. M. to his daughter in the grocery store.

"Can you believe this is how my father still talks to me?" she asked in my office.

"How do you feel when he talks like that?" I asked.

"All of a sudden, I get very scared. I feel like I'm a little girl all over again. But I remember what we talked about and I realize that he can't really hurt me anymore."

"So what do you do when he talks like that?" I continued.

"At first, I kind of freeze up. Then I remind myself to start breathing. Then I just make believe I never heard what he said and I don't respond at all."

"What would you like to say to your father?" I asked.

"One of these days," responded Therese, "I would like to come right out and tell my father, 'Dad, that's a completely inappropriate way for a father to talk to his daughter.'"

"You have every right to tell him exactly how you feel," I encouraged her. "Whenever you feel comfortable enough, speak up for yourself."

"Yeah, but he'll go crazy," she responded fearfully.

"In the grocery store?" I asked. "No, he knows better than that," I added confidently.

"Yeah, you're right," she replied. "He's not so brave in front of other people."

Six months later, Therese's mother got so ill that she passed away. She was devastated. Her mother had not always been available to meet her needs and she had always failed to protect her daughter from her father's abusive behavior, but Therese realized that her mother was unable to even defend herself throughout her marriage to Therese's father, much less her daughter. Therese identified with her mother's sense of powerlessness and she could forgive her as much as she could forgive herself.

When her mother died, Therese's father was overwhelmed. He didn't know how to let friends and relatives know what had happened. He didn't know which funeral home to call or how to make arrangements for the wake or burial. So Therese stepped in and took control. In spite of her own grief, she spoke up and made all the phone calls and all of the arrangements.

Mr. M. was shocked to see his "little girl" doing what he could not. For a few days, their roles had reversed. He was dependent on her to get through this difficult period of his life. Mr. M. was now in his late seventies and he was able to do less and less for himself.

The transition of their roles lasted beyond the days of the funeral. Therese continued to help her father organize his bills and his budget. She also helped take him to the store more often. Mr. M. clearly appreciated the love and dedication that his daughter demonstrated.

More time passed and Mr. M. grew increasingly lonely. There was no one else at home and he longed for companionship. But his crude demeanor hadn't changed. He still had not learned how to talk to women, particularly his daughter.

"I don't know what I'm going to do," Mr. M. admitted to his daughter while shopping one day. "Since your mother's been gone, I'm tired of talking to myself."

"I understand, Dad," replied Therese compassionately. "Maybe it's time you started dating. After all, Mom's been gone for over a year now."

"Yeah," Therese's dad agreed. "It's been a long time since I've been with a woman... In fact, it's been so long I think my balls are turning blue."

"Dad," reprimanded Therese. "That's no way for a father to talk to his daughter." (Therese and I had rehearsed this conversation many times before.)

"Whadda ya mean?" replied Therese's dad. "You know what I'm trying to say."

"Yes, I know what you mean," she responded. "But there's a more appropriate way to talk to your daughter. You could just say that you're 'ready for companionship' or that you want to have 'intimacy with a woman again.'"

"Oh," remarked Mr. M.

At this point, Therese realized that her father really never used words like "companionship" and "intimacy" when he was growing up in his own dysfunctional family. On her father's side of the family, they always talked at each other and competed with each other. As one of the younger boys in a large family, Mr. M. never got his share of his mother's attention. Instead, he learned to use "machismo" to make a name for himself. He obviously had his own lengthy history of abuse and neglect.

This realization further validated Therese's impression that her father's sick, sexual behavior was a product of his own upbringing and underlying sense of inadequacy. His attempt to show any love for a woman was always expressed in sexual terms. He had never learned a safe, sensitive way of expressing himself. It did not excuse his sexual abuse of her as a child, but Therese was able to see it as a problem separate from her personal integrity. This distinction helped her to separate her father's sexual aggressiveness from his underlying, but apparent love and appreciation for her. This distinction also helped Therese to separate her experience of sexual victimization from her awareness of real love between a father and his daughter—the love that she had longed for forever since she was a child. Therese had always felt that her father loved her dearly, but he never seemed able to communicate it to her without her fearing there were strings attached. In session, Therese started commenting that "he seems more and more like a lost little boy who needs someone to love."

This larger awareness became a cathartic experience.

Therese was finally able to understand why her father behaved the way he did, why she no longer needed to feel threatened or victimized, and how she could start to forgive her father for traumatizing her during those many childhood years. She now felt more confident and less afraid; forgiving her father helped her to move forward in a positive direction, rather than being "held captive" by the past.

Additionally, since their roles were now functionally reversed, Therese was in the powerful position of teaching her father how to act appropriately, so that she could enjoy a healthy relationship with him for whatever years they had left together.

Mr. M. very much appreciated all the time and patience Therese offered him, particularly since his wife died. He saw his daughter as a strong, competent woman. He began to ask for her advice and trust her opinion on a variety of topics. He even started to confide in her about his fears.

"You know I hate being alone," Mr. M. confided to his daughter.

"Yeah, Dad, I know," replied Therese.

After a brief pause, Mr. M. continued, "I don't even know where to start."

"What do you mean Dad?"

"Well, I don't know if another woman would think I'm good enough."

"Why do you say that?" Therese asked.

"I've slowed down a lot. I don't feel strong like I used to."

"Dad, you don't have to be strong. You just have to be nice," she instructed. "A woman just wants the man to be nice."

"I don't know if you understand what I mean," Mr. M. persisted. "I don't know if I'm up to sleeping with another woman."

"Yeah, I figured that's what you meant," Therese replied, taking a deep breath. She felt bold enough to continue, "You know, Dad, maybe you should just worry about becoming friends with a woman— before you worry about sleeping with her."

A look of sadness came upon her father's face. "But why would a woman want me if not to sleep with her?" he asked, apparently thinking he had no other worth.

"Dad, a woman could be your best friend first," advised Therese. "A friend to talk to, laugh with... someone with whom you could enjoy real companionship. Whether you sleep with her or not is secondary."

She had her father's full attention. Then he started to cry. "Therese, you are my best friend. You are my lifesaver. I don't know what I would do without you."

Therese always hoped she could be this loved and appreciated by her father. By sorting out the history of her own abuse, she was able to let go of the hurt and find hope in her future. She was able to forgive her father and actually reconstruct her relationship with him. She showed her father what it is to give unconditional love. By healing her wounds, Therese was able to find a healthier way to relate to her father, as well as all of the other men in her life.

4

Paula:
Being Sexually Violated...
and Then Finding Your Power

There was a clear gap between Paula and Bobby and it was growing wider every day. When they were first married, it felt to them like they were best friends. Each one was ready to listen to the other with a great deal of compassion and understanding. Their sexual relationship was once also very exciting and they couldn't wait to find time to be intimate with each other. But now those intense feelings were fading. Their friendship and intimacy was suffering. Neither Paula nor Bobby was feeling happy anymore.

Paula spent many months complaining about her husband. He was rather quiet. He was often preoccupied with his work, which left little attention for Paula. Paula's needs were not being met. Her body language told me even more: usually her head was lowered and her shoulders were slumped over. When our eyes met, I could feel her pain. But the pain seemed very deep and very old—even older than her relationship with Bobby.

In therapy, I gave Paula my undivided attention. But often, she would not talk. She seemed preoccupied by something going on inside. When she looked up, I asked her what she needed. She did not respond. She didn't seem to know. It was clear that there was much more that needed to be addressed—but how? I asked Paula more and more details about earlier relationships. She offered more information, but she would only give me "hints" about the most painful memories. "I'm not ready to talk about it yet," was all she could say.

Paula's predominate feeling was fear that if she let it all out, she would fall apart. But holding it in was suffocating her. She was only in her twenties, yet she always felt weary and lifeless. My feeling was that if Paula didn't get this pain off her chest, she would go into an even deeper depression. I told her that I understood this dilemma. It was very, very hard. I had even experienced it several times in my own life. I told her that I knew from both professional and personal experience that talking about your worst experiences was painful, but that it was more painful holding them inside. Once your feelings were out in the open, there was always a way to make sense of them and find peace. Holding feelings inside just made a person feel separate and alienated from everyone. Paula understood.

So she tried to talk more, but at a pace that helped

her to still feel "in control." Each week, she spoke a little more, her voice quivering and her eyes glossy. Paula made reference to being abused several times since being a teenager, but the details were often glossed over. I prodded her for more information, but she was clear about not being ready yet. Often, a couple of tears would run down her cheeks. But she could never let herself have a real cry. For now, she had to hold back. It was too dangerous.

My eye contact was comforting to Paula—but then it would suddenly feel dangerous to her. I told her that it would be perfectly fine if she felt safer writing her feelings on paper before or after a session. Then when she came to the next session, she was free to choose how much of her letter she felt comfortable about sharing with me.

One week Paula came in looking a little more self-assured. She walked in with her posture more upright and her steps more exact. As she sat down, she looked up and gazed directly into my eyes. "I have something for you," she proclaimed, and she reached into her pocketbook to grab a letter. "You can read it all," she added, placing it in my hands.

I would not know until much later how much faith, courage and fear were mixed into this moment. The faith was understood. The courage was apparent. But the fear was immense. Paula's breathing was shallow and her heart beat like it was coming out of her chest.

Paula was to become emotionally naked. With her defenses totally removed, she was vulnerable to any judgment I might make. She felt ashamed of herself and her lack of foresight, judgment and experience. Would I, a professional whom she had come to respect, now tell her what a fool that she had been? Would I tell her how stupid she was to get into so many dangerous situations? Would I, at the end of a long list of authority figures, tell her that she really was crazy to have gotten herself into so much trouble? Would I compound her guilt by telling her that she somehow brought all of this upon herself? But the worst fear she had was that maybe I would conclude that after all of her "experimenting" with sexual feelings at an early age, she deserved all of this pain.

When I held Paula's letter in my hand, I did not know how much fear raced through her veins. On the contrary, I felt only compassion and gratitude. Her letter felt like a gift of trust and of faith, an invitation into her life. I felt that a connection of spirit was being made.

"Dear Rich,

I have often thought about how I was going to go about doing this and I feel most comfortable writing it. It's the best way for me to get out all the details. Whenever I picture myself doing this, whether I picture it being in your office or in a letter, I find it easiest to start from the beginning. Some of this I have already told you about, other parts I don't remember if I have or not, or to what extent. So here goes:

In January 1980, I had my experience with Victor. Between sixth period biology and seventh period social studies, Victor grabbed me in the stairwell of our junior high school. He told me that he wanted to molest me. I don't even remember if I knew what molest meant. The next thing I remember was being pushed up against the wall and Victor had his hand against my throat. He then kept grabbing at my body, telling me that this is what girls were meant for, and that he intended to get "it" from me. I remember trying to fight him off and telling that he was full of shit. Whenever I tried to block his advances, he would slap my hands and once or twice my face. He didn't let up and he kept telling me that this would be all I was ever good for in life. I remember thinking he was wrong. I don't know how much time had passed during all of this, probably not nearly as long as it felt. When Victor heard someone enter the stairwell from the lower level, he let go of me and I fled. I went to my class and told my teacher that I had to go to the principal's office to take care of something. I wanted to make sure that he didn't do this to someone else. What if the next girl didn't get away like I did? I don't even want to think about what would have happened if that person hadn't entered the stairwell when they did. Next thing I knew, I was sitting in the principal's waiting room. I had to wait for what seemed like an eternity. When I finally got into Mr. Bower's office I told him that Victor attacked me in the stairwell. He asked me what I meant by attacked. I told him that Victor kept grabbing me. He then asked me where Victor grabbed me. I was too embarrassed to name the parts of my body that were touched. Bower asked me if Victor touched my breasts. I told him yes. He then asked me if my buttocks were grabbed. Before I could answer him he said, "That's your rear end, honey." I said that I knew what the word meant and that yes, I was grabbed there as well. He then called Victor down to his office and asked him what had happened. I can't remember what Victor said. Bower basically said that it was a misunderstanding and that maybe I had led Victor on in some way. He told Victor not to grab girls anymore—that was it, end of story. I couldn't believe what I had heard. I felt so defeated. I never told anyone about this for years. I was afraid to tell my parents for fear that I would be punished. When I think about this, I get more angry with Bower than with Victor. After all, I felt that he should have known better being an adult and having a degree in education. I wonder if he knows what he did to me making me feel that I was to blame. Sometimes when I picture the scene in his office, I'm there as a thirteen year old girl, telling my story and also, I'm there as an adult saying to Bower, "What the fuck is wrong with you?" I still can't get over how he made me feel. It was almost as if he agreed with Victor about a woman's purpose. I don't really remember much after that except I didn't want anyone to touch me in any way, for any reason. It wasn't until about three years later, when I started dating Eddie, that I knew touching could be nice and comforting.

Eddie and I started dating in our first year of high school, twelve years ago. We went to different junior high schools, so he didn't know about the Victor incident. Eddie was very popular and a lot of girls liked him, including me. I was so shocked when he wanted to date me instead of any of them—(There's that self esteem thing again). Ours was a typical high school romance—sweet sixteen, dances, ankle bracelets, first time you say and/or hear "I love you," the whole deal. It was so weird for me to be loved in that way. For the first time in my life I felt important and cared about. I eventually told him about Victor, mainly because people in school were talking about what they believed had happened. Since I never talked about it, no one knew the truth. They just knew something had happened. Eddie was very understanding about the whole thing. For the first time I did not feel that I had done anything wrong or anything to provoke Victor. When Eddie and I broke

85

up, I took it very hard. My parents didn't understand why I was so upset since to them, this wasn't real love, only puppy love. I know now that back then I didn't have a real understanding of what love was because the love I felt for Eddie was nothing compared to how I feel about Bobby, but it still hurt when we broke up.

When I was nineteen, I started dating Tim. We worked together at Burger King. He was more insecure than I was. I'm not sure if he loved me or just the fact that he had a girlfriend. I'm not so sure that I loved him either. I cared about him, but I wasn't in love with him. I think I saw him as a way to get away from my family. I don't think that I really was aware of this while we were dating. I think I realized it later on.

After we got serious, I told him that I was told by a couple of doctors that I probably could never have children. Though Tim said he still loved me, he told me that his mother (who never thought I was good enough for her son) advised him to forget about me and find someone else. In fact, there was one time that she said something nasty and it started a big argument between us. Tim was standing right there but he remained silent. He wouldn't speak up to his mother. In fact, when I tried to question him about it, he just got quiet with me. He then broke up with me. I felt so hurt and alone.

A few days later, Tim came back and said that despite this, he loved me and wanted to spend his life with me. He told me that I was lucky because not many guys would want to get serious with a woman who could not have children. I believed him. I think the reason I stayed with Tim, other than to escape my family and the fear that no one would want to get serious with me, was because he thought I was beautiful. I wasn't used to guys thinking that about me. In school I was always told how smart I was (and made fun of for it), but never that I was pretty. My brothers always told me how ugly I was. It was nice to hear differently. Even though I had many signs that I shouldn't marry Tim, I still made all my wedding plans. One sign was that I had no real desire to sleep with Tim. I thought that was really weird, especially since I had agreed to marry him. I thought about sleeping with him, but more because I felt embarrassed being a virgin, not because I wanted to make love to him. Tim was a virgin, too, and somewhere along the line we agreed to wait until out wedding night. I think that that was as long as I could put him off without him finding out that I really had no desire for him. I wonder if I would have married Tim if his mother and I hadn't gotten into that big fight. As much as it hurt to hear her say all those mean things to me, I'm glad it happened because it forced me to call off the wedding.

After I broke up with Tim, he called me constantly, day and night. He would even follow me around and show up where I worked. He always begged me to come back to him. We got back together once, for about two weeks, but broke up again. He then started calling me again and following me. He even told me about plans to kidnap me. I told him that if he didn't leave me alone that I would call the police and have him arrested. He finally stopped bothering me. That was about six years ago.

After I broke up with Tim the second time, I started dating Matt. We met at Hofstra University. He was a political science major and wanted to be a lawyer to help low income families get legal counsel. We seemed to have the same dreams about changing the world. I remember talking to him for hours after class. Eventually we started dating. He told me that he had never met anyone like me. He told me that I was unselfish and genuine and that I had a good heart. He seemed to be caring and giving. He loved animals and children and wanted to help people who were less fortunate. I guess I fell in love with that image of him. I kind of refer to that person as "faux Matt." After we were dating a couple of months Matt told me that his ex-girlfriend had aborted their baby. This was when he told me that falling in love with someone like me, who may not be able to have children, was his punishment for the abortion. As much as it hurt to hear that, I guess I believed it to be true. After all, I should consider myself lucky that *he even considered getting serious with me in the first place. Soon the issue of sex came up. Being a virgin at twenty-two was something that I always felt I had to defend. If any of my friends found out that I was a virgin, they would always ask why, like there was something to explain. I didn't believe that it was necessary to wait for marriage, but I wanted to wait for someone that I loved and with whom I felt I had some sort of future. I just hadn't met him yet. I was never interested in having numerous lovers, in fact I really only wanted one true love forever. That was my ideal fantasy. Matt made me feel embarrassed that I was a virgin and kept putting pressure on me to sleep with him. I considered it because I was afraid of being alone and, in my eyes, I already had two guys who were willing to "settle" for a woman who would not be able to give them a child; I didn't think there would be a third. We made plans to sleep together. I wanted a romantic evening with champagne, candles, and soft music. He agreed to that, but when the night finally came, I chickened out. I was so afraid that it would hurt and I was afraid that I would not know exactly what to do. Matt was upset with me, like I led him on. A couple of nights later was when he raped me. We were at his parents' house. No one was home. We started to make out and Matt wanted to take it further. I told him that I wasn't ready yet, that this was not how I wanted our, and my, first time to be. The next thing I knew, he was on top of me, pulling at my clothes. I was crying and telling him to stop. For a moment I was back in the stairwell of my junior high school and Victor was saying, "See Paula, I told you that this was all you would be good for— to fuck." I remember screaming out in pain when he entered me. I had never been in so much pain before. I felt my flesh tearing. When he was finished, he got off me and I ran into the bathroom. I fell to the floor and started sobbing. I remember being very cold and shaking. Then I realized that I was bleeding. It wasn't the same as when I would get my period, but rather like cutting yourself with a knife. Matt knocked on the door and asked what was wrong. I told him that I was bleeding. He said, "Well, virgins bleed." I don't remember what happened next. I don't even know how I got home that night. When I did get home, I went inside my bedroom and started to cry. My parents were away for a couple of weeks, so I was alone. I went into the bathroom and noticed that I was still bleeding—and heavily. I started to get worried. I had to stop the bleeding. I tried applying pressure, but I was still bleeding pretty heavily after about twenty minutes of doing so. I knew that I probably needed stitches. I didn't want to go to the hospital for a few reasons. One, I didn't feel strong enough to drive to the hospital; I also didn't want to explain why I was bleeding from my vagina. I also was under my father's insurance and I didn't want him to get a bill from the hospital for this. I then came up with the idea to do the stitches myself. I still can't believe that I actually thought about giving myself stitches, let alone actually doing it. I remembered that when I was a candy striper at the hospital I had taken some of that dissolvable thread that they used. I found it, boiled it, boiled a needle, took a mirror into the bathroom, and gave myself a couple of stitches. I think I threw up and then cried myself to sleep.*

I didn't yet define what had happened as rape. I felt that I had failed and that there must be something wrong with me. I didn't break up with Matt at this point. He acted like nothing unusual had happened. I didn't tell him about the stitches; I just told him that I was too sore to have sex. After a couple of weeks he would just start to have sex with me whenever he felt like it. I never tried to fight him off and each time that we would have sex I would just lie there waiting for it to be over. I felt so used and worthless. Matt treated me like I was an object; he only cared about his own pleasure. I was in physical and emotional pain each time that we had sex. Matt said that the physical pain would lessen over time and that the emotional pain was my own problem and that I should just "get over it." I guess I felt that I was stuck with him. No one would ever want me now. Here I was, this twenty-two year old girl who couldn't have kids and was horrible in bed. I wasn't even good at the only thing I was supposed to be good for. I just wanted to die. I began to realize that I had been raped. I guess it was hard for me to recognize that before, since Matt was my boyfriend. I decided not to press charges. I was afraid of a repeat performance of Mr. Bower's office. I also had no witnesses and Matt was my boyfriend. I think I also believed that maybe I had led him on since I did agree to sleep with him once before. This was five years ago. To this day, whenever I get out of the shower, my legs and arms are red from me scrubbing them vigorously to get rid of the filth. Bobby and you are the only other people who know about this.

I started to date Bobby the following year. When we got on the subject of sleeping together, Bobby told me that he was a virgin. He was waiting for the right person, too. We talked about how other people made us feel like weirdoes because of this. I fell in love with him and loved him like no one else before. I knew that I wanted to be with him forever. I felt that he was that one true love I had waited for. I told Bobby that I was not a virgin, but that I had been raped. I didn't give him any details about it. I also told him about Victor. Bobby was so understanding and he seemed to be angry for the way I had been treated by Matt, Victor, and Mr. Bower. When we made love for the first time, it was everything that I had ever hoped it would be. In my heart, that was when I lost my virginity.

After I was raped, I had nightmares all the time. The whole incident would play over and over in my mind. It seemed so real. It wasn't like I was remembering what had happened, but rather that the rape was actually going on at that moment. I would actually feel cold and be in pain. I would usually wake up screaming at the same point where I had screamed during the actual rape. The nightmares continued for few months and then stopped after I met Bobby. Recently, they started up again—I'm not sure why.

This was the easiest way for me to get some of this out, Rich. I didn't have to worry about running out of time or not being able to speak about it once I was in your office. I was always afraid of starting to talk about it and not being able to finish and then I would be left dangling. I don't know what I am looking for regarding the rape. With the problems that Bobby and I have, I know what I am looking for. Maybe that's why it is easier for me to talk about them.

Paula"

Paula told me later that as she watched me intently read her letter, she expected me to be shocked and dismayed about her "sordid" past, as she described it. The greater part of her braced herself for a lecture about how she "should have known better" and how she somehow "deserved" the consequences. This message (in its many forms) is what she always got.

Instead, I was feeling very moved by what I had just read. There was so much in my hands to react to and my own emotions briefly overwhelmed me. Once again, my initial reaction was predominately one of gratitude—for this young woman taking the chance to show me so much of her inner self. This was indeed a gift.

When I looked up, Paula was looking down. Her eyes avoided mine. I could feel her shame and her fear of my reaction, so I proceeded to speak very softly and gently. "There are no words to describe what you've been through. It's no wonder that you have had such a hard time trusting anyone when you have been hurt and betrayed so many times. I am particularly grateful that you took the chance to trust me—a man."

Paula later confided to me that my voice was reassuring and comforting. It was a masculine voice unlike others from her past: non-threatening, not condescending, non-judgmental. My voice was soothing and it allowed her healing to begin. It was a connection of deep empathy. It was the calling of a kindred spirit. It was then that Paula felt strong enough to sit back, pick up her head, and look up to allow her eyes to briefly meet mine.

Maybe there was no need for shame. Paula had always believed that somehow she had brought all of this upon herself. Maybe she had somehow "misunderstood" Victor's intentions in the stairway. Maybe she had somehow misunderstood "a woman's purpose." Maybe her difficulty in conceiving children was a "curse" or punishment. Maybe Paula deserved to be raped because she didn't believe it was necessary to wait for marriage to have sexual relations— contrary to what her parents had said.

Now that all of these internalized beliefs were out in the open, they could be carefully reviewed and reconsidered. Initially, the process was very intense and very painful. As Paula sobbed in my office, I often thought to myself that I wished there was some way to console her and quickly "make it better." But her healing had to come from within. Her psyche and soul had to mingle, grieve out loud and find healthier ways to integrate these experiences. How did these things happen? Why would a young woman have to endure such trauma? What were life's lessons to be learned? Between tears, Paula began to make sense of this mess. After several weeks, she began to find peace of mind.

Paula realized that she may have used poor judgment at times, but that she had been young and naïve. She may have made some poor choices, but overall, her victimization had not been her fault. Once she was able to write and speak openly about these experiences, she was able to pinpoint exactly how she had let others' beliefs pre-empt her own.

"I thought I was the crazy one," exclaimed Paula. "Mr. Bower was a fucking idiot. I would like to meet him now and tell him how incompetent he was." In another session, she proclaimed, "I can't believe that Tim thought he was doing me a favor by going out with me... And do you know, I once heard his mother calling me 'the barren bitch'? Now I feel sorry for the two of them."

The rape was particularly difficult to review. This is when Paula felt the most pain, the most loneliness and the most shame. The image of a young woman stitching herself together on the bathroom floor is one that neither one of us will ever forget. But great desperation reveals great strength. By reviewing this as a twenty-seven year old, she could recognize her internal fortitude.

Paula began to see that she had been able to survive all of these traumas with great personal strength. By recognizing exactly what had gone wrong in each of the situations, she could see now that she would never let it happen again. By reviewing each experience in detail, she was able to specify how she would now be able to effectively handle each situation. Paula was able to explain how she would now utilize and execute her personal power.

The freedom to talk openly, about anything, was a cornerstone of that power. Paula was able to start talking openly with her husband about what she needed and expected from him. She no longer felt awkward and embarrassed when she had to talk to Bobby about sex. In fact, the roles reversed. Bobby became the one who found difficulty finding the right words to express himself.

After months of reviewing her early history, Paula had a newly discovered confidence and sense of womanhood. Her perspective of Mr. Bower, Victor, Tim and Matt changed as well. She began to see all of them as smaller and weaker than she had ever been. In fact, a part of her began to feel sorry for each of them. Each of these men was confused and weak— so much so that they had had to bully a young woman in order to enhance and sustain their egos.

Now that Paula could recognize and exercise her strengths, she was in a position to forgive her abusers. She did not excuse their behaviors, but she was ready to give herself permission to let these traumas join part of history. The events no longer interfered with her daily functioning. The sick behavior of her perpetrators inhabited only themselves-not her. They alone would suffer from the consequences of their actions. They would suffer until such time that they sought help for their own confused lives.

5
Lenny:
Trauma... Finding Reassurance
After 9/11

In September 2001, I was busy working with several children and their families in two New York City schools, trying to help complete several diagnostic evaluations. On September 11, 2001, I was one of many millions who were shocked and saddened by the unfolding events of that day. Both adults and children were confused and scared, and even though our school was located far from the World Trade Center, the adults in the building tried to reassure each child that they would be able to get home to their families safely and securely.

The next day all New York City schools were closed. The following day was the first day back to school after the terrorist attacks. Our school in Queens was several miles away, but more than one child told me that they could see the smoke in the sky as the site continued to burn. Enormous fear continued to fill the air. All of New York was on High Alert and we all walked around in a kind of daze, wondering if the terrorists had planned another target to strike.

I, the school social worker, was on call for any teacher who may have needed help with any of the fifteen hundred children in the building. I also intended to be available to any of the teaching staff that may have had a hard time coping with the chaos. But what about my own emotions? Who was there to support me? I am not sure. Maybe a deep faith. Maybe a voice deep inside. Maybe my guardian angel.

The staff as a group was connected by an inner spirit of unity and strength. We were determined to lead the way for the children. We knew how important it was to provide a sense of normalcy and safety for the children. We made every effort to put our own fears aside for the moment and give our children a sense of stability in a time of great crisis.

The first day back to school, I patrolled the halls to find out where I was needed most. One teacher stopped me and expressed her deep concern about one of her students. This was a class of five-year-olds who had just started kindergarten one week earlier.

As I walked to the doorway, the teacher directed my attention to Lenny who was sitting quietly on the far side of the classroom. The other children were very animated in play typical of five-year-olds, but this little boy was eerily silent. He sat still, his eyes gazing into the air.

At this point, I did not know whether Lenny had

lost someone, maybe even a parent, in the WTC attack. I gently asked him to accompany me back to my office. Almost mechanically, he walked alongside me until we reached my door. Then he sat down, still quiet, with his eyes open wide.

"You seem worried," I commented. Lenny looked at me and nodded.

"Tell me why you are worried," I continued softly, hoping that he would feel comfortable enough to explain his feelings.

"We're going to blow up," the child explained.

"Why do you think that?" I queried.

"I saw it on TV. They're knocking down all the buildings. They're going to kill us next," Lenny proclaimed.

Apparently, he had watched the constant news coverage of the terrorist attacks. He watched Towers One and Two being hit by planes, from different angles, over and over again. In Lenny's mind, different buildings were being destroyed each time. Soon, all of the buildings, including our school, would be destroyed. Lenny was just waiting for all of us to die at any moment.

I reassured Lenny that what he saw were only two buildings being attacked. He just happened to see it replayed over and over again. But the boy's fears persisted.

"When the two pilots hit the two buildings, they

died too," I reassured him. "So they will not be able to hurt anyone ever again," I added. I knew that much to be true, though I didn't know what, if anything, the next few days might bring.

I watched Lenny process all of this new information. His contorted expression gradually gave way to a wave of relief. He looked up at me, and smiled for the first time.

"I can't wait to get home," he announced.

"Why?" I asked.

"Because I have to tell Mommy the good news. She's been crying for the past two days and this will make her happy."

6

Patti and Brett:
When The Honeymoon Ends
In Three Months.
Re-Igniting the Spark of Passion.

Patti called me to set up an appointment. I could hear the sadness in her voice. Her speech was labored and I could tell that she was depressed. She and her husband Brett were having serious marital problems.

"How long have you been married?" I asked.

"Next week will be our three-month anniversary," she grimly replied.

"I'm sorry to hear that," I commented, with no sense of surprise in my voice. "I talk to a lot of couples who don't know what to expect when they get married."

"I can't believe it." Patti exclaimed and she started to cry. "We were engaged for two years. Then this past year, planning the wedding was a lot of pressure." She regained her composure over the phone. "That's all we did. Plan for the wedding. The church, the hall, the gown, the dresses, the limos and everything else."

"Then we had to pay the hall forty-thousand dollars.

We had to take money out of the envelopes on the wedding night to finish paying off the balance," Patti continued.

"I can see that you both must have been under a lot of pressure," I said. "So I can see how your marriage may have 'gotten off on the wrong foot.' People tend to think that 'love' will just magically make everything work out after the wedding vows. But it just doesn't work that way. What you didn't get a chance to talk about before the wedding always appears soon afterward."

"So you don't think we're going to get divorced?" Patti asked, revealing her worst fear.

"No, not at all," I reassured her. "We just need to meet together to go over the list of issues that have not been addressed properly and have built up over the past several months. Then the plan would be to take one issue at a time and try to resolve it."

"Oh, I see," Patti responded optimistically. "So how soon can we meet?"

A few days later, I got to meet Patti and Brett in person. Unfortunately, it was apparent that the tension in the relationship was very high. Patti walked into the office with her head low. She seemed to be carrying the weight of the world on her shoulders. Actually, she was dragging Brett in just behind her.

It was clear that Brett did not want to be there. He looked very unhappy and his eyes rolled upward as he entered. I could almost hear his thought: "What the hell am I doing here?" But he managed to turn his smirk into a half-hearted smile as he reached out to shake my hand.

The next few moments would be very telling about their relationship. I watched where they sat. (Next to each other or on adjacent couches?) Would they make any physical contact while talking? (Holding hands or touching feet?) The two of them proceeded to sit on the same couch and each of them surreptitiously reached out for the other's hand. This was a good sign.

"So what brings you here?" I asked, opening the conversation. Patti spoke first, which didn't surprise me.

"I'm not happy. It seems that Brett and I fight all the time. But we fight about a bunch of stupid things." I looked over to Brett for confirmation. He made eye contact with me and nodded his head.

"It's not that we don't love each other," Patti continued, "and it's not like Brett does anything terrible. He doesn't hit me or cheat on me. He's actually a very nice guy. He volunteers at church, helps a youth group. And he's a good friend. He helps people move. He helps fix their cars."

"So what's the problem?" I asked. Brett looked at me again, this time with his eyebrows raised, very much approving my question.

"He doesn't talk to me enough," Patti said. "He doesn't pay enough attention to me. He's always busy."

"One minute," I interrupted.

"I know, I know, it's silly," Patti blurted out. "If I told any of my friends that this is why I insisted that Brett go with me to marriage counseling, they would tell me that I was nuts. One time, I complained about Brett to a friend of mine who had been married for three years. She told me, 'That's how married life is... Brett's a nice guy, so just count your blessings and stop complaining.'"

I corrected Patti: "I interrupted you not because I thought you were silly. Obviously, there's a reason that you and Brett are not getting along and there's a reason you're feeling miserable. I interrupted you because I wanted a moment to grab a piece of paper. I wanted to make a list of all the problems you started to describe." Then I looked over to Brett, "Next, I'll be asking you for your list. After all, that's only fair."

Brett nodded in agreement. "Yes, that would be fair."

"Once I have both of your lists," I continued, "I'll have a good idea about the overall theme of the conflicts you describe. Then we can prioritize the lists and work out each problem, one-by-one. After several weeks, you'll be able to see how most of these problems may be resolved rather easily," I added, with great optimism.

I turned to Patti with a pen in hand. "Okay, let's get back to your list. Just tell me whatever comes to mind and I'll write as fast as I can. Don't worry if it seems vague or whether you've forgotten anything. We can always add to the list later. We're just using this list as a starting point."

"Okay, here goes," Patti said.

"He doesn't seem to care about me. He never wants to hear about my day. "

"He tells me that I am overreacting - that it must be 'that time of the month' again."

"I don't feel important to him."

"He never wants to discuss our problems."

"He doesn't tell me what's bothering him."

"He shuts me out."

"When a football game is on, I don't even exist."

"Brett doesn't stick up for me with his family."

"We don't make love like we used to."

While Patti was telling me what is bothering her about her relationship with Brett, I did three things. First of all, I quickly understood from the theme of all of her complaints that Patti was feeling very neglected and unloved. She knew intellectually that her husband loved her, but it seemed that he was behaving in a way that was inattentive and unloving. And the last item on the list, "We don't make love like we used to" was a big "warning sign." The way in which a couple makes love is usually a good barometer of the direction of the relationship.

The second thing I did was listen to Patti's complaints without judgment or criticism. Unlike the times when she had confided to her friends, I heard her pain. I understood why she was so unhappy and depressed. Who wouldn't be in that situation? I told her that these complaints were very common, not at all unusual. I wanted Patti (and Brett, too) to feel at ease. Many times a couple in pain or crisis will look at other couples and think that everyone else is doing okay. They will think that their problems are so unique and odd that they feel like outcasts. I reassured them that nothing could have been farther from the truth.

At the same time that I was listening to Patti and reassuring her, I also kept my eye on Brett. I looked to see if he was shocked or surprised by anything she had said. None of it seemed like news to Brett, but I could see that he was not comfortable listening to her complaints. While I was sure that Patti had told him all of this before, Brett had never had to hear it in a setting like this one. People are generally not used to having forty-five minutes of uninterrupted time to spend on their relationships. In a session, there are no phones ringing, no televisions on and no children crying—common things that might get in the way of a couple communicating. I could imagine the thoughts running through Brett's head:

"Oh great, I get dragged to this stupid session. My wife is painting this ugly picture of me and this therapist guy is reassuring her. I'm screwed."

I wanted to put Brett at ease. I was there to help him,

not judge or reprimand him. I asked Patti if she had finished. As much as I wanted to reassure Brett, I did not want Patti to feel cut off or neglected in any way. When she had finished, I turned to Brett. I looked at him without judgment and asked how he was doing. I wanted him to feel safe and to see that I was not going to jump down his throat and verbally attack him.

I then invited Brett to share his list. I told him that I was sure Patti was not perfect and that he, too, may have some complaints, issues, or concerns about their relationship. I told him that even if he didn't have any complaints, there may have been things that he felt could be done to help improve the marriage and make it better.

Brett struggled to give me a list. I could see how he took great effort to choose each word that came out of his mouth carefully. I could tell that he had been afraid to bring things up to Patti in the past. What if he said something to upset her? What if she overreacted to a criticism? By me not judging Brett or verbally attacking him after Patti spoke, he could feel safe to bring up his issues and concerns. He started to believe that he would be heard and understood.

Brett started to tell me a few things:

"Patti should know that I love her."

"She has to repeat things over and over again. Doesn't she know that I heard her the first time?"

"I'm tired when I get home from work. I can't be

bombarded with stuff the second I walk through the door."

While Brett was speaking, I nodded my head in understanding. This encouraged him to add more:

"I get annoyed that Patti gets so emotional and upset."

"Why does she cry so much?"

During all of this I was listening to Brett as he probably had never been listened to in his entire life. I was hearing what he was saying and I was letting him know that he was not wrong for his feelings. I told him that I, too, worked a lot of hours and was often tired when I got home. I understood the feeling of not wanting to be bombarded when I walked in through the door. I validated his frustration and annoyance.

I was also watching Patti while Brett was giving his list. She was not shocked by the complaints that her husband had, but I could see that she was a little taken aback by the realization that this wasn't all about her pain. He was feeling pain, too.

Brett's list was much shorter than Patti's, but it was much broader. He felt that he was in a no-win situation. If he tried to talk to Patti about what was bothering him, she got upset and hurt, so he didn't bother talking at all. He felt helpless and got upset, too.

At this point, Patti and Brett were feeling equally helpless. They were also upset and confused. Neither of them understood why it should be this way, especially when there was no big reason why they were having such trouble in their marriage—(no cheating, no physical abuse).

I asked, "What happens at home when you try to discuss these issues?"

Predictably, Patti was the first to respond. "As soon as I start to bring something up, I see that 'look' on Brett's face and he just starts to turn me off right away."

"I don't like the way she says things," Brett retorted, "It's 'you don't do this' and 'you don't do that'. She never talks about what she does."

Patti interrupted, "It doesn't matter what I say. You don't respond to me at all."

Brett disagreed, "When I try to explain why I did something, that doesn't satisfy you. You just go on to the next thing, then the next thing after that and eventually I just give up. It's a no-win situation."

She defended herself, "So I'm always wrong and you're always right. Is that what you think?"

"Now you didn't hear what I said. And you always exaggerate and make the problem worse than it is already. That's why I get so angry. It's better if I don't say anything."

"What do you mean?" Patti asked.

"Sometimes I get so frustrated that I'm afraid that I'm just going to call you a 'bitch'—and then we'll really have an argument."

I completely understood why the two of them were unable to discuss anything. And I knew why they had become miserable with each other after only three short months of marriage. It was time to intervene.

"Now it's your turn to listen to me." I began by congratulating them for coming to therapy. I immediately saw two surprised faces looking at me. I let them know that yes, they had heard me correctly. I explained that seeking help was a good thing. I told them that the fact that they were seeking help early rather than later in their marriage was also good. It showed that they cared about their relationship and valued it. Why else would they be trying to save it? I explained that it was good to be proactive and resolve things before deep resentments set in. (It is one of my pet peeves that there is no law requiring couples to get counseling—even just one session—before they get married. I know that many religions require some form of counseling or classes on marriage, etc., and that is great, but unfortunately this does not happen for many couples. And in Brett and Patti's case, they needed more than what was covered in their Pre Cana classes.)

I told them this to help take away the stigma of therapy. If one is hurting physically, he or she would go to the doctor. Why doesn't the same hold true for one who is hurting emotionally?

Going back to their lists, it was clear that many of

Patti and Brett's issues related to communication—or rather, the lack of it. I told them that I was going to give them some new communication skills to try during the week and that we could review how it went at our next session. I gave each of them a sheet listing the top ten marital communication skills.

THE TOP TEN MARITAL COMMUNICATION SKILLS

1. Attempt to talk about your problems in a relationship. Suppressed feelings will inevitably undermine love and intimacy in a relationship. (Men tend to withdraw—women tend to emote or get depressed).

2. Listen closely to your partner's concerns and don't interrupt until he/she is finished.

3. Stay on one issue. Don't try to address a second issue until the immediate issue is resolved.

4. Be honest and accurate in your statements and responses. Don't exaggerate your own statement or discount your spouse's.

5. Stay in the present. Do not rehash the past. Don't project into the future.

6. No name-calling—direct or inferred.

7. Stay with "I" messages rather than "You" messages. Talk about your own feelings and actions—not your partner's.

8. Feelings and desires are not "right" or "wrong." Avoid these judgments. Instead, respect the other's right to an opinion—even if it is the opposite of yours. Avoid blanket "black and white" statements. Most issues are variations of gray.

9. If either one of you cannot help being "seduced" into a fruitless argument, be the first one to detach— temporarily.

10. Be the first one to reach out and reconnect. It is courageous—not a "weakness."

IF YOUR PARTNER DOES NOT FOLLOW
THE ABOVE, YOU DO IT ANYWAY.

As Patti and Brett started to look at the list, I said, "After working with many couples, I have found that it's good to have a concrete guideline available for use in between sessions. I suggest that you put this list in your pocket, inside your kitchen cabinet door, or even right on the front of your refrigerator. Then when you try to discuss something, talk with each of these rules in mind. If you can say what you have to say while abiding by these guidelines, you should be able to eliminate ninety percent of your communication problems."

I let Patti and Brett take a few moments to look over the list and try to imagine following the suggestions. The room was quiet. The two of them became speechless. Brett started to look fidgety. He realized that this "counseling stuff" would drag on for more than forty-five minutes. "The homework is going to be even harder than the class." Patti browsed the list and began to laugh.

"What's so funny?" I asked.

"I'm trying to imagine making it past number two," she wisecracked.

"Oh, I have faith in you both," I said with a chuckle. "This will be fun." I added, "There is a big advantage to working on this as a couple, as a 'team.' When you discuss something, you can help each other stay on track and be productive—and maybe be able to resolve whatever the problem is, once and for all. And even if your partner doesn't follow the rules, you must follow them anyway. Then you get to be considered the 'healthier' person when it comes to communicating."

Patti seemed to like this challenge. Brett seemed to be ready to go home. But he admitted that if Patti overwhelmed him next time they had a discussion, he liked being able to point to number four or number five as a response instead of getting quiet and angry.

I told both Patti and Brett, "The goal of marriage counseling is more than just being able to have a good discussion. It's about getting all the nonsense out of the way so that you can feel your love again."

I saw that we were out of time, but I felt that the first session had been productive. Both of them seemed to be exhausted, but they also seemed to be more hopeful and communicative than when they had walked in.

At our second session, Brett and Patti walked in looking less tired and they made more eye contact.

"How was your week?" I asked.

"Better," Patti responded.

"Okay," remarked Brett.

"Can you be a little more specific?" I prompted, looking from one to the other.

"When I brought things up, Brett usually stopped what he was doing and listened to me," Patti added, hopefully.

Brett agreed. "Yeah, I really tried to be more patient and I tried to talk more myself."

"That's good," I said. "The secret to a long-lasting marriage is good communication. People usually think the best predictor of a successful marriage has mostly to do with how much you have in common. People believe that agreeing on the same kinds of things is what keeps couples together. But the fact is that the way in which people handle conflict is the best way to predict whether two people will stay together."

I took it a step further by adding, "Think of it this way: Any couple is bound to have a major conflict or argument about any number of things, particularly once they start sharing the same household. If they cannot find a way to resolve one or two of these major conflicts, then the marriage is at risk. However, another couple may have dozens of areas in which they disagree. If they are able to discuss each of these conflicts in a way that respects each other's feelings and needs, then they are likely to grow closer with each conflict, not farther apart. With each discussion, a deeper insight and understanding results and the couple is able to proceed, even closer than before. In this way, arguments actually bring blessings to a relationship. They are opportunities to bring discontent and unmet needs to the surface so that they may be resolved. Without this opportunity, these feelings are likely to fester like an untreated wound, resulting in misunderstanding, resentment and eventual alienation. Then love gradually erodes away."

Brett and Patti listened intently, nodding in agreement that this might just make some sense.

"In fact, the people who don't seem to ever fight may be at the greatest risk. I've come across many couples who preferred to pretend that everything was fine—only to be shocked that one's spouse had been keeping some deep, dark secret or had been acting out some hidden desire for several years before being discovered. But by then, unfortunately, too much damage has been done and it is much harder to salvage the trust between them and the relationship itself.

"So let's start addressing your specific issues," I said, moving on. "I have both of your lists from last week. Let's take another look at them and start working on them."

"I'm ready," Patti said.

"Okay, me too," Brett added, somewhat less enthusiastically.

I decided to start with Brett's list, hoping that would help to "bring him into the fold." I looked at him and commented, "I have your list in front of me. Where do you want to start?"

"It doesn't matter," he replied meekly.

I decided to pick an easy one: "Let's see; how about 'I'm tired when I get home from work. I can't be bombarded with stuff the second I walk through the door'?"

Brett smiled. "That's a good one," he replied.

I turned to Patti, "What do you think? Is this request unreasonable?"

"But you don't know how he is," she objected. "I've tried waiting until later. I wait until dinner, but he doesn't want me to upset his meal. I try after dinner, but he doesn't want me to interrupt his television show. It doesn't matter when I try to talk to him—he never wants to hear it."

"Don't start," Brett interrupted. "You see what I mean?" he added, turning to me.

"It looks like we're getting into other parts of both of your lists," I observed. "Let's back up a minute. I hear Brett saying that the worst time to try to discuss anything is right after work."

He nodded his head. "I'm still wiped out from work and I've got to unwind a little when I get home."

"That's understandable," I commented, validating Brett's feelings. "What if you agree to try not discussing anything important with Brett until at least one hour after he comes home?" I turned to Brett, "Then you would agree to pay serious attention to Patti anytime after that. That would be the 'deal' between the two of you. Does that sound fair?"

Both of them nodded their heads.

"Good, we have just taken care of one item on your lists."

Brett interjected, "But if I agree to this, then what do I do if later she 'starts' and doesn't know when to quit?

"So I see we're talking about some of the other things on your list," I acknowledged to Brett, "like 'she has to repeat things over and over again' and 'I get annoyed that she gets so emotional and upset.'"

"Well, I wouldn't have to repeat myself if you would only say something the first time I asked." Patti said in her defense. "I'm so tired of you ignoring how I feel, and when you finally answer me, you say something really mean like 'it must be that time of the month again.'"

It was time to interrupt again. I turned to Patti to validate her feelings this time. "If Brett is the 'strong, silent type,' I commented, hoping to add some light humor to this debate," then I can understand why you may think that repeating yourself may increase your chances of being heard. But I'm sure he hears what you have to say the first time you say it." I raised my eyebrows as I turned toward Brett, and he simultaneously nodded his head.

I told Brett, "It seems that when Patti repeats herself several times, she might get increasingly frustrated and more emotional. I imagine that she may sometimes even start to cry or scream."

"Oh, yeah," he agreed.

"I have an idea." I continued, "If you agree to make a point of responding to Patti the first time she says something at least one hour after you get home from work, then we'll see if Patti is able to be calmer about what it is she has to say to you."

"That sounds good," Brett said.

"It will be nice to have a real conversation at dinner for a change," Patti responded sarcastically.

"As we draw near the end of our second session, it seems like we're starting to make some progress on your lists," I told them.

Both Patti and Brett agreed.

"Is there anything else we need to go over before we finish for today?" I asked them.

"No, I think we're pretty set," said Brett.

"Yeah," added Patti, "this has been a good session."

Over the next several weeks, Patti, Brett and I were able to discuss not only how to communicate, but what to communicate. We were able to discuss more and more meaningful issues surrounding the relationship. The couple was able to fondly review how they had first met and what had quickly drawn them together. They were able to review and reignite the early attraction they had toward each other. The connection and intimacy they shared was described as "good fortune" and a "rare blessing" once again. Emotional ties blossomed and the excitement was reflected in their love life. Both Brett and Patti reported that their lovemaking was more frequent and more intense than ever, and they were grateful.

As several months passed, we explored more and more about the individual personalities that made up this precious relationship. Brett's constricted style of communication was similar to most of the men I knew. It also reflected my own father's pattern and the way in which I myself was raised.

In my family, we were raised not to share our feelings. Masculinity was always defined, in part, by seeing how much you could hold onto. Charles Atlas could hold (an image of) the world on his shoulders, and as men, we always believed that we could do the same.

In our modern society, all of our role models are "strong" men. Whether they are in sports, the military, politics, business, music videos or the movies, men always function well in spite of whatever it is they may be feeling. It is the tough men who succeed in all areas—not the kind, sensitive men. It is also the "bad boys" with their own agenda who seem to attract the most women and who seem to be the most loved. Being cold and aloof is portrayed as being very manly. Men who are warm, passionate and open with their feelings are made to feel like freaks. They are considered "weak" or "gay" by most of the media. They are also considered to be the minority that can't measure up to society's recognized standards.

As a therapist, I am privy to the big secret among men: We are overloaded with lots of feelings and we fantasize about having a best friend, male or female, with whom we can confide. Without such a friend, no one may ever know the pain we're in, unless of course you happen to be around when we are very drunk or very high and we lose all control over social expectations.

So how does a tough, sober man love his wife? A "real" man "protects" his wife by not bothering her with his problems or concerns. A "real" man walks around with a bad back or a sore neck, "loving" his wife by "shielding" her from the tension he feels. For the "real man," the prototype is the strong, silent type.

Don't ask a "real man" what he feels. He'll just bypass the issue and jump right over to what he can do for you. That's why it may not seem that he is listening to what you need. Listening and relating to how you feel may trigger all kinds of anxiety, fear, and awkwardness in a "real" man. It is much easier to try to buy you something, perform a task or just give you the advice that you should do something to feel better. But as a woman, you may already know that all that men really need to do for them is just be able to share their feelings with someone who can simply listen and then respond in kind.

As a young boy, Brett had learned how to "be a man" by following society's role models. But more importantly, he had learned the specific "how to" rules from his father. He had learned how to communicate and how to address conflict in the family by the consistent, frequent examples he had observed.

Brett's father found it "safe" to avoid dealing with his mother's complaints as much as possible. It was "safe" to just go along with whatever his mother had to say. It was even "safer" not to talk about anything that may pose a conflict. So Brett's father appeared to be a pleasant, cooperative man most of the time.

But predictably, Brett's father could bear only a certain amount of frustration before his voice and demeanor would reveal his real sentiments. Then his voice would suddenly become louder, an argument would follow, and sooner or later, he would just get up and walk off in bitter hopelessness. A temporary "truce" would take place between Mom and Dad—until the next time.

Brett had learned well. He was able to reenact the scenario perfectly within his own marriage to Patti. The pattern was automatic. It was safe. It was manly. But it felt shitty. Just like when he was a boy.

Brett hated how he had felt as a boy. He spent years feeling trapped in a volatile, unhappy household. Day after day, he had dreaded the same arguments being replayed, sometimes word for word, week after week. He tired of moving to the furthest parts of the house where the arguments could scarcely be heard. He was sick of going out to the street or to a friend's calmer house to find solace. He swore to himself that once he got older and could escape this torment, he would find a way to live in peace in his own house.

When Brett found Patti, she was calmer and more peaceful. She was looking for a way out of her family patterns also. Brett was determined to be a better person than his father. He was determined to have a better marriage than his parents'.

Patti was a woman who wasn't afraid to express her

feelings. She liked expressing warm, loving feelings the most. She made it safe and easy for Brett to open up and share some of his feelings for the first time in his life. Loving someone else became safe for the first time.

Brett enjoyed falling in love. Unlike his father, he could say, "I love you" and even "I'm sorry" out loud. He knew that when he had gotten to know Patti, he had found a "soul mate" for life. She was truly a blessing to him. With Patti, Brett was excited and happy. He felt very much alive. It wasn't until after they were married that life's changes started to accumulate at a faster pace. Having a new household of their own was both exciting and overwhelming.

It was at about that time that Patti's expressive nature presented a challenge to Brett. Part of him wanted to hear everything that she wanted to say. He sincerely wanted to be a "good" husband. But another part of him was feeling overwhelmed and scared. As a man, this was next to impossible to admit out loud. So he started to get quiet - for protection, for self-preservation and automatically, without even realizing it... just like his father.

Over six months, Brett and I were able to explore and piece together this whole process. It was painful to go over the history. It was exhausting to map out the dynamics. But it was exhilarating to discover the sense of it all. Brett's internalized dysfunction could be carefully externalized and understood. Once the actions and reactions were nailed down, he gained the "tools" he needed to make some conscious choices about what kind of man he wanted to be.

Of course, Patti had her own family history, which was also being replayed in the relationship. She was the youngest of four children. One might guess that as the "baby" of the family, she received an inordinate amount of attention from the rest of the family. However in reality, Patti was the most neglected.

There were at least two reasons why Patti's needs were constantly overlooked. Pete, her next older sibling by three years, was the "shining star" of the family. He was extremely bright and he almost always got straight A's in his studies. Patti's parents were always very proud of him. Pete was also pleasant and cooperative. He never got angry or challenged his parents' authority. He was almost a "perfect" child.

As Pete reached his teen years, he entered junior high school and he continued to do well academically. His teachers were also very pleased by his diligence and his academic performance. But Pete started to work a little too hard at being the best scholar and the best young man. He started to exhibit increasing signs of anxiety and despair. Pete continued to excel academically, but emotionally he became increasingly fragile.

By high school, Pete didn't feel like he "fit in"

RICHARD C. SCHEINBERG, LCSW, BCD

at all. He became socially phobic. He buried himself in his books as a way to hide from the world. Pete's parents continued to commend him on being the top student in his class, but the teenager became severely depressed and completely withdrawn. His parents were deeply concerned about him and they spent months—and then years—taking him from doctor to doctor, seeking the right combination of medication and psychotherapy to alleviate his deep depression.

In the meantime, Patti was growing up as the fourth child of parents who had precious little energy left to spare. They did the best they could, but they resorted to the "traditional" rules of childrearing when it came to little Patti. She would not be a child who was "spoiled" or over-indulged. She would be a girl who should not whine or complain or demand too much attention. Pete had already consumed most of the time and energy they could offer and they were exhausted.

Patti got the "message". She should not expect her needs to be important. In fact, there was no reason for her to be upset about much of anything. She came from a fine, hard-working, intact family. The two oldest siblings seemed to have grown up fine; they had gotten married and had moved on with their lives. Pete, their third child, was always a good boy who studied hard, but he unfortunately had succumbed to some kind of "mental illness." Patti needed to understand the importance of "doing the best she could" and succeeding like the first two had done.

To Patti, this felt like neglect. The life script she had been handed left no "liner notes" about what to do with the inevitable "ups and downs" she would experience in her young life. The message was that unless she too was mentally ill, she had nothing to complain or cry about. As a very young child, she learned to keep those feelings to herself.

Patti recalled a vivid incident that occurred when she was only four-years-old. "I had this bookcase in my room that I kept my toys in. One night I was trying to open the bottom doors on it when something from the top shelf fell and hit me on the head. I was bleeding quite a bit and started to cry. My father screamed at me from the living room to 'knock it off.' I remember being so scared that he was going to come in my room and spank me, but I just couldn't stop crying. My head hurt so badly and I was scared of all that blood. My father just kept yelling at me to 'be quiet' and that he 'didn't want to hear it.' No one came in to check on me to see if I was okay. It wasn't until much later that he finally did come into my room."

As I heard this story, I remember thinking how sad it was for that four-year-old girl to have gone through that alone. "How terrible that you had to feel so alone at such a young age," I expressed to Patti.

"Yeah. Now that I think about it, that really sucks that no one bothered to check on this little kid—me—

who was probably screaming at the top of her lungs. I mean, when you cry out in pain, it is a lot different than whining. I remember that night so vividly... It hurt like hell. I needed stitches to close the cut, so that tells you that my injury was no little scrape."

In my office Patti, for the first time, felt entitled to feel and express her anger, which was rooted in early experiences of neglect and pain. This lesson about the "outside world" was to be repeated over and over again in the years to come.

Patti recalled another major incident that she described as a "turning point" when she was only ten years old. She had a very close relationship with her grandfather. He was one adult in her life who was emotionally available to her from time to time. "I remember coming home from school one day and my mother was packing her suitcase. I asked her what was going on. She told me to sit down on the couch. I remember feeling sick to my stomach, like I knew something bad was going to happen. My mother just looked at me and said, 'Grandpa died last night.' I couldn't believe what she had just said. I asked her what had happened. She told me that Grandma called last night from the hospital to tell her that Grandpa didn't make it through the surgery. I remember thinking to myself, 'What surgery?' I didn't even know that he was in the hospital. I asked my mother why she had sent me to school that day if she already knew Grandpa had died. She just told me that it was better that way so I wouldn't have to miss any more school than necessary. She then told me to pack my navy blue dress and enough clothes for two days because we had to go to Connecticut for the funeral. I remember crying the whole time, but she never put her arms around me. At the funeral, it was as if I wasn't even there. Everyone knew that Grandpa and I had a special relationship but no one said anything to me. No 'I'm sorry Patti'—nothing. I know my mom was sad about losing her father and that Grandma was sad about losing her husband, but what about my sadness? Didn't my feelings matter? I remember feeling at that moment that I had my answer: No, they did not."

As Patti told me about her grandfather, the tears flowed from her eyes, but it was apparent that she was anxious to have her story heard rather than taking the time to pause and reflect on her sadness. Now that she had finished, she looked up me and our eyes met for the first time. There were tears in my eyes, too. It was clear, without words, that I had heard her and that I could feel her pain.

So by the age of ten, Patti had been taught over and over and over again to keep all "negative" feelings to herself. She had no right to whine or complain. If she dared to verbalize any of these most personal experiences, she would get no response. Even worse, her words would not even be heard.

But the human spirit cannot be suppressed. It must be heard. It must find the connection that it knows intuitively to exist. To deny such a spiritual connection on the Earthly plane is to invite mental illness. Like Pete had done years earlier. Patti spent many years in "emotional silence," but she never gave up her spirit. She harbored her present feelings deep inside, but her "bold statements" were made in other ways. Patti used her keen intellect to develop smart retorts, sarcasm and humor—and of course all of it was safely directed outside of her family. As a teenager she had also made herself known by her brightly colored outfits and "big" hair, which was sometimes streaked blonde or purple. Though still an "A" student, she was considered to be the most rebellious of the four children. And she was silently proud of this reputation.

Patti dated several men through her late teens and early twenties. She always fantasized about finding the right guy—a guy she could talk to, who would listen and respond. She knew that there must be someone "out there" with whom she could finally share her deepest feelings- feelings she had not dared to share since she was ten.

Then she finally met Brett. Initially, he was rather shy and quiet, but Patti's keen wit and outgoing nature helped to draw him into long conversations. Their personalities complemented each other well. Each one had found a kindred spirit.

Long talks led to both Patti and Brett being able to "bare their souls" to each other. A bond formed quickly and romantic feelings followed. Sexual feelings came easily and effortlessly. For the first time for each of them, lovemaking evolved without awkwardness or shame. The couple found that their physical "rhythms" mirrored their emotional harmony and this was deeply satisfying. After six months, Patti and Brett talked seriously about marriage. A few months later, they announced their formal engagement to the world.

As stated earlier, the "work" created by planning a wedding took its toll on this couple. Both of them worked full time jobs and their free time became increasingly committed to visiting catering halls and flower shops rather than spending their time sharing common sentiments.

The couple fantasized that they could finally resume their "real" relationship after the "wedding event" was over, but they were never able to recapture that earlier "magic." The stress of setting up a new apartment, painting and buying furniture with the wedding money created new ways to keep busy. The time when hours and hours were spent sharing love and life still lay beyond reach. After a few months, the unrelenting stress prompted each to return to old, familiar coping strategies. Brett got quiet again.

Patti started keeping her feelings to herself. Until this whole process was revealed in therapy.

Now that both of them were able to identify exactly when their feelings of anger and neglect had originated and now that they were able to see, after a year, how they had almost lost their sacred connection when "tested" by much stress, they were able to salvage the spiritual sparks that had brought them together in the first place. Patti and Brett chose to focus on the positive, precious connection they had made and nearly lost.

In the last few months that brought closure to the therapy process, Brett and Patti were able to recover all of the intimacy that had been there all along. The accomplishment of being able to gain an even deeper appreciation of their spiritual connection after both histories of anguish and despair made each feel even more blessed than before.

The couple believes that they have survived the "darkest hour" of their union. They now have the faith that their relationship can withstand any adversity that they may have yet to encounter in the years to come.

7

Diana:
Love Taps...
Reacting Sooner than Later

Diana was frantic on the phone: "My husband and I need an appointment as soon as possible. Do you have an opening?"

Rather than ask her to wait while I checked my appointment book, I asked immediately, "What happened?"

"We were driving in the car and we started to argue. After about ten minutes, we began yelling at each other. And then..." she paused.

"And then what?" I prompted.

"Then he reached over and hit me on the head," she replied.

I could hear the embarrassment in her voice.

"I mean, I never expected this from him," she continued. "I waited a long time to find a decent guy. I'm almost thirty now... I've known him awhile now. He's always been a quiet, gentle, caring guy... I never expected this."

"How long have you been married now?" I asked.

"Three weeks," Diana replied. "We just got back from our honeymoon."

I was surprised. "There were no previous signs that he could act out his anger in a physical way?" I asked incredulously.

Diana paused for a moment. "I don't think so," she replied, though she now seemed to be asking herself the same question.

"How could that happen?" Diana continued.

"When we meet, I can help you both figure that out. But for now, I can tell you that people do act a little differently once the marriage vows have been said. The idea that you have a commitment toward each other usually gives each individual permission to act out a little more than before, without fear of being rejected. Sometimes that acting out may be a good thing, in the sense that the individual may be more openly and directly compassionate; however, at other times, it may be a bad thing. An individual may take more liberty acting out in a negative way if he or she feels that 'you won't go anywhere now.'"

I didn't elaborate on the phone, but I knew from past experience and formal research that this behavior is not to be taken lightly, even if it happened only once. Some people may think that Diana acted prematurely by immediately seeking a professional to intervene, but often the first "incident" is a test to see if acting out physically on your spouse will be "understood" or "excusable" when you're angry. In fact, what often happens is that when the first signs of domestic violence are tolerated, it is predictable that more serious transgressions will follow in time. (In my childhood, I witnessed several of these incidences.) So Diana is to be highly commended for making this phone call and taking a firm stand on what is acceptable and healthy early in her marriage.

Wisely, Diana told her husband immediately, "I don't know what got into you, but you better not do that again!"

"I wouldn't have done that if you didn't make me so mad," was his attempted defense.

"I don't care how mad you are," Diana retorted. "If you ever hit me again, I'm outta here!"

He knew there would be no excuses for this behavior.

"In fact, we will have to see a marriage counselor so you can figure out what got into you."

"That's okay, we really don't have to... I'm sorry, Diana. It'll never happen again."

"I don't want to take any chances," she insisted. "When you can figure out how you did such a thing in the first place, then I'll believe you."

"Okay, I'll go if you want."

"Yes, I want. That's a definite. If we are going to be together for the next fifty years, I have to be able to trust that I can have an argument with you without having to be afraid that you might hit me. I have a few girlfriends who are afraid to speak up to their men. I don't ever want to feel that way about you."

8

Mary:
She was Always Attracted to the "Bad Boys"

On a hot summer day, I stopped at a deli to pick up a bottle of water. It was late in the afternoon and I was the only customer in the store. A lone young woman waited behind the counter as I searched the glass cases for my selection. With the bottle in one hand and the other searching for my wallet, I approached the counter. As I got closer, I couldn't help but notice tears in the young woman's eyes.

"Are you okay?" I couldn't resist asking.

"Yeah, I'm okay," she responded glibly.

"No, really," I persisted. "Are you alright?"

"Well, no, not really. But it's a long story."

Since we were still the only two people in the store, I continued. "What do you mean?"

"Oh, my boyfriend and I had this huge fight and now... he tells me... he doesn't want to see me again." Tears began to roll freely down her cheeks.

"I'm so sorry to hear that," I said, as I tried to console her. "Hopefully, you have someone in your family or a good friend you can talk to."

She looked up, paused and said, "No, not really."

At this point, I debated about what to do next. Should I talk to her a few more minutes and then leave? Should I tell her that I'm a therapist and give her my card or would that be unprofessional? I also wondered if this was just a coincidence that I had happened to get thirsty and enter the deli at this exact moment or whether this was some type of fate? Or even divine intervention? My experience had taught me that there were really no coincidences.

I decided to go with my gut feeling. "We can talk for a few minutes now. But I want to let you know that I happen to be a psychotherapist," I said with a bit of a smile.

"You're kidding me," she replied.

"No kidding... as I said before, it would be nice if you had someone in the family or a friend to talk to about this, but if you really don't have anyone, I would be glad to plan some time with you." I pulled a business card out of my wallet and handed it to her. What to do next was now her decision rather than mine.

We talked a few more minutes and then I told her that I needed to be on my way. "Oh, by the way, what's your name?" I asked her.

"Mary," she replied.

"Hi, I'm Rich. Nice to meet you," I said. We both

couldn't help but chuckle at the irony of having such a brief but intimate conversation as virtual strangers.

By the time I arrived at home, my secretary had left me a message that a new client, "Mary," had wanted to set up an appointment. I was still fascinated about the sequence of events that brought this about, especially since I had just finished with a client one week earlier—leaving only one opening in my schedule. The opening also happened to be on the very next day. I returned Mary's phone call and set up the appointment.

Mary came to the office and it was immediately apparent that she was still quite upset and shaken. She was lost in her sadness and confusion. I wanted to learn more about this "wonderful" man that she had lost. "Tell me more about this guy," I prompted.

"Well, he's a very interesting guy... he belongs to this group."

My eyebrows rose a little. "What kind of group?" I asked.

"A motorcycle club," she replied.

I was tempted to question her judgment, but I held off asking the obvious questions.

"He's a tough guy with a bad reputation," Mary admitted, "and I wasn't even attracted to him at first. But once I got to know him, I started to see that he wasn't so bad after all."

"Where did you meet him?" I asked, wondering if

perhaps he had stopped by the deli as well.

"I met him and his friends on a Saturday night at my other job," she explained. "I also work at a bar to make extra money when they need help.

"I used to be afraid to talk to bikers," Mary continued, "but after getting to know them better, they seem a lot like everyone else who comes to the bar. Bryant would stay until three or four in the morning. He liked to tell me all kinds of stories. The bar would empty out in the early hours, so we would get a chance to talk a lot. Also, after a few drinks, he used to tell me a lot of things about himself that he didn't tell anyone else."

"So you started to feel very special."

"Yeah... I realized that he had a sensitive side that no one else knew about."

"So you wanted to hear more and more."

"Exactly... So we started seeing each other outside of the bar."

As we talked, it was evident that Bryant could only be "sensitive" when he was drinking. Otherwise, he was often crude, controlling and defensive. Mary could admit this out loud. She also knew that he was demeaning and sometimes abusive. She understood intellectually that it was an extremely unhealthy relationship. But she was "emotionally addicted" to it. She had seen a glimmer of feeling behind that tough exterior and she was determined to keep "digging" for it, even if she acted masochistically in the process.

It was clear that Mary was subconsciously looking to find closure for an old, familiar fantasy. I decided to explore a new "path" with her "Tell me about your father."

"We were never very close," she confided, predictably. "He owned a business and we were very well off. But he worked a lot of hours and we never saw him until the weekend. But even then, he always seemed to have a lot on his mind. Me and my sister could never quite figure out how to get his attention."

"So you are used to working hard to get some attention from a man," I reflected back to her.

Mary knew what this meant.

"You're used to earning the love you get," I added, reinforcing this new insight.

Tears filled her eyes. "Yes. I can't believe how hard it was."

"You need to know that you are a wonderful person who deserves to be loved for nothing more than being who you are."

"What?" Mary responded, with a puzzled look.

"You need to be less hard on yourself. You need to appreciate your own qualities and love yourself just as you are."

She gazed into my eyes, trying to absorb this information deeply into her psyche.

In later sessions, I expanded on this notion. "I'm sure that there were plenty of men before Bryant who cared about you without you having to work so hard for it."

"No, there weren't."

"I can't believe that," I challenged. "Think all the way back—even to high school. So far, all the men you've dated have had obvious signs of being tough, hard-to-reach men. In fact, you seem to be an expert at finding cold, detached men. So now I want you to really stop and think about the "others." The ones to whom you never paid any serious attention."

This time, Mary paused and thought a few minutes. "You know, there was this guy Jason."

"Yes. Go on."

"He was a smart kid in my class. He asked me out to eat and to the movies in my senior year in high school."

"What happened to him?"

"We went out a few times. He was always very nice. We talked a lot... He always wanted to know what I was doing and what plans I had when I finished school."

"And...?"

"And one time he even brought me a rose when he picked me up."

"So what happened?" I continued, curiously.

"Well, he was kind of too nice. It was overwhelming," Mary admitted. "I didn't even know what to say to him when he asked me so much about myself... After all, I never really thought much about me and what I planned to do."

"So you didn't find him very attractive," I conceded.

"No, I didn't," she replied regretfully. "He just didn't seem like a *real* man." As the words came out of her mouth, she wanted to take them right back. "I know," she said. "It's sick."

Mary sat for a few moments, amazed with this new revelation. All of a sudden, getting Bryant back into her life didn't seem so important anymore. She realized that "winning Bryant back" or "winning anybody over" to be loved was not the only way to have a deep and meaningful relationship with a man.

We discussed the fact that there would always be early signs in each relationship that she could use to predict the ease or difficulty that might be experienced while working to sustain the relationship. There would be many choices to make. And the choices that affected her life were really hers all along.

9

Carol:
Falling in Love with Someone
Outside of Marriage

After meeting with Carol for a few months (as detailed in Chapter Two), she was able to find consistent relief from her deep depression and occasional suicidal thoughts. Then Carol was ready to talk to me about Bill. He was someone with whom she could open up, someone who saw the potential in her. She said that it wasn't planned; she and Bill just "connected" in a way that felt "special", but at the same time, felt very confusing. As described earlier, Carol told me that she and Bill started talking at work and then they started having lunch together. They were able to talk about "everything".

"Lunchtime goes very fast... I feel like we could keep talking for hours."

"Well then, that makes a lot of sense," I proclaimed.

Carol was puzzled. "What do you mean?"

"Here's a guy you can talk to, about anything for hours—and you have so much to say. Why wouldn't you find that to be an attractive situation?"

Growing up, Carol was used to keeping her feelings to herself. Her mother and father both worked full-time and there were six children for them to raise. They often depended on their daughter to look after her younger brothers. As a "parentified child," there just seemed to be no opportunity for her to get all the attention she needed and craved. So Carol settled for limiting her attention to the special recognition she received as the "good" child upon whom Mom and Dad could depend to keep the household running smoothly. Her special role helped her to feel a little less alienated in her family.

When Carol met "Carl," she finally began feeling very special and loved. They married within a year and Carol gave birth to her first child a year later.

Though Carl was anxious to become a father, he had some difficulty with the increased responsibility and greater financial pressure. 2:00 A.M. feedings and working overtime hours made him feel like weeks were going by without him getting enough proper sleep. Carl became more stressed and even though he was exhausted, he started having difficulty falling asleep. He found that having one or two drinks before bedtime would help "relax" him enough to get some sleep.

Two years passed. A second child was born and Carl had developed a serious drinking problem. Carol tried to talk to her husband about the problem, but he didn't like to talk about it much. He just told Carol that she was over-reacting and that he could handle this problem by himself. After that, she spent many nights crying herself to sleep. A familiar feeling returned. Once again, Carol began feeling alone and unhappy in her family.

Two more years passed and a third child was born. Fortunately, the year before, Carl had finally agreed to go to Alcoholics Anonymous to stop his drinking. The couple got along much better, but Carol had gotten in the habit of keeping her deepest feelings and worries out of their daily conversations. She feared that a highly charged confrontation might knock Carl "off the wagon" and she could not take the chance of going through that hell all over again. Carol kept her deeper emotions confined to conversations with her few close female friends; however, she kept her most intense and confused emotions completely to herself.

Carol knew that her husband really loved her as deeply as he could love anyone and that fact gave her solace. Carl continued to work hard and he was a good father to their children. From the outside, family and friends believed that the two of them "were back on track" and appeared to be happy.

Carol believed that her family was good. She and Carl had weathered difficult times, which seemed to have brought them closer than she believed her own parents had been in their marriage. She believed that this was the best she could hope for—until she met Bill at work.

Carol would talk to Bill about things that her husband didn't want to discuss. They would talk about the kinds of issues she had previously saved for her gatherings with girlfriends. They would talk about traveling and museums. They would also talk about movies—even "chick flicks." Bill wanted to hear about all of it. If a topic was of interest to Carol, he wanted to know about it. "The more we talk about anything, the better I get to know you," he explained. It wasn't long before Carol wanted to tell Bill about everything. And lunchtime was just not enough time with him.

Initially, it may have seemed that Bill's infatuation with Carol was due primarily to her being a friendly, young and attractive woman, but it soon became apparent that he was going through a very difficult period in his own life. His wife was preoccupied with the children and redecorating the house. He was overwhelmed at the hospital trying to keep up with his duties as a physician's assistant, but he was never able to find the "right time" to get his wife's attention to talk about these concerns. She, in turn, resented Bill putting in so many hours at the hospital. She felt that Bill was not home to spend enough "quality time" with her and the children. Their last argument ended with "We had better find a marriage counselor," but neither Bill nor his wife took the initiative to pick up the phone.

Once Carol was able to disclose how deeply meaningful this was and how much Bill validated her, how she found him mesmerizing and attractive, and how it was such a joy to speak with him about things that her husband refused to discuss, it was very clear in my mind that if this relationship was not yet sexual, it would become so. Weeks later, Carol confided to me that she and Bill had romantic feelings for each other and that some things had been done that she felt very guilty about. When she confessed this information, she expected to be reproached. She expected me to chastise her in some "therapeutic" way. She almost demanded it from me. Carol was feeling so much guilt about her relationship with Bill that she wanted me to tell her directly that it was just plain wrong.

It was apparent that the guilt was so overwhelming that Carol had problems sleeping at night. Over the past week, her depression and turmoil had become so intense that she wrote the following letter, which she just handed to me, her eyes focused downward in shame:

"Here I go again. Just when I thought those feelings were gone, they're back. I just want to die. I just want peace and I don't know how to get it. Can't kill myself, won't kill myself. Wouldn't do that to my daughters. They're the only reason I won't. I feel

trapped, I feel isolated, I feel stupid, really stupid. My insides are churning and my brain feels like it's going through shock treatment. My thoughts are so jumbled and I feel I'm at a low, low point. I fight and I fight with my own self to try to get better but I can't. I have no identity. I'm bad. No one can help me. God won't. Why I continue to pray to this savior, I don't know. He's not alleviating my pain. He's not helping me to see anything. Even if he is, I'm probably just too stupid to see it. I don't know how to think on my own. I never did. I just did whatever I could to make people like me and continued on that path. I hate the fact that I need to be accepted and liked in order to feel good. I don't know how to think on my own and whenever I do, I get knocked down. So I stop. God, I feel so trapped that I can't breathe. I don't know who Carol is. The Carol I know is weak, she lacks direction. She lives in a maze that she can't get out of. She trips over herself.

I don't know what to write about next. It requires me to go too deep. I want to drive myself to the hospital to admit myself because I feel like I'm going to have a nervous breakdown. Maybe that's what I'm having right now. I'm exhausted. I haven't had a good night sleep in weeks. I keep the TV on to distract me from my hell. The television is the only way I can fall asleep. There's no way I could fall asleep without the television on. Too much going on in my brain—

the TV distracts and calms me.

When I get into moods like this, I just want to run away from home and go talk to Bill. He knows that I try to be a good wife, a good mother, a good friend and a good worker. But I just can't keep up with all of it. When I get all confused about it, Bill seems to just listen and he seems to understand. He looks at me, deep into my eyes and he says that he understands. He says that he gets depressed sometimes himself. He knows how I feel and he wants me not to feel so bad. He says that he would do anything to make me feel better. That's when I just want him to take me in his arms and hold me. I want him somehow to save me from this pain. When he holds me close, when I lean my face on his neck and shoulder, when my skin touches his and I breathe in his scent, I feel a little better. I can relax in his arms and forget about everything else, even if it's just for a little while.

But then I have to go home. I know the right thing is to try to talk to Carl about how miserable I feel. He's a good guy, but he never knows what to say. I try to explain my confusion to him, but he doesn't really let me finish. He seems to get impatient when I'm upset, and he just tells me not to worry so much or not to make such a big deal about it.

Now that I think about it I really don't want to rely on my husband or anybody else for that matter for my happiness. I want to be able to rely on me and me alone. I just wish I knew how....

I get scared for my daughters. I know they love me because I tell them and I physically show them, but I know I confuse the hell out of them. Kayla and Diana are less of a concern than Sarah. Sarah concerns me. She seems to me to be a little girl lost. However, she is unwilling to find her way back. It's too much work for her. I feel like I confuse the hell out of her. I feel like I have damaged her—a lot—and I can't save her. I don't know how to talk to her because she's so hard to reach.

Sarah reminds me very much of Carl. They have similar exteriors. It's hard to get through to them both, but it seems their insides would ooze out if their exteriors were broken down. The both of them are the hardest to connect to.

I'm tired now, it's gotta be between 2:00 & 3:00 A.M. Hopefully I can sleep."

Again I purposely passed no judgment. I continued to ask Carol the significance of the relationship with Bill and what she was getting from it. She continued to be shocked that I hadn't condemned her about all that she had revealed to me. Sometimes she verbalized again that she "was sure" that I must have thought less of her. Even when I tried to reassure her verbally, she accused me of looking at her differently.

"No, my gaze is not to judge you—it's just a

pause to "feel" the confusion and shame you must be experiencing."

"Are you sure you don't hate me now?"

"Yes, I'm sure. You are the same woman I liked just a few weeks ago," I jokingly replied.

Several weeks later, Carol raised the issue once again: "Bill and I are getting more and more involved with each other. But then when I get home I start feeling guilty about the whole thing. Then I wonder whether I should just quit my job and try to forget the whole thing... I don't know what to do. What do you think I should do?"

Once again, I would not take responsibility for Carol's decision. Other clinicians may disagree about me not taking some type of stand about this dangerous situation. Others may attempt to "protect" a client in some way from "inappropriate" attempts to satisfy needs, but I prefer not to direct the client at all. The client really needs to decide for him or herself what is best.

If I advised Carol to stay at her job, at least two possible scenarios could take place: (1) She could continue to lead a "double life" without having to make any conscious choices (studies show that as much as 50% or more of all married people have affairs and lead "double lives" for some period of time). This way, she could "keep her family together" and remain "financially stable," while simultaneously getting her emotional and sexual needs met outside of her marriage. (2) By being confronted daily with this dichotomy, Carol may feel forced to make a choice: try to let Bill go and work on her marriage or leave the marriage (and ask Bill to leave his marriage) and try to start a new life. Either way, Carol would need to know what her choice to stay would entail and whether or not she was ready to face this risk by choosing to stay.

If I advised Carol to go ahead and quit her job, then at least two more scenarios could take place: (1) She might find peace and comfort by physically distancing herself from Bill and then focusing her energy on trying to get all her intimacy needs met within her marital relationship. (2) On the other hand, breaking away from Bill might represent the loss of an established, loving relationship that could never be replaced. The loss of such a potential source of comfort and happiness could prompt Carol to plunge into her "black hole" of depression. Would she want to risk having that feeling again? Again, after reviewing all of these options and their implications, Carol herself would need to make the decision in her own best interests.

These were only four of dozens of possible scenarios and Carol worked very hard by exploring, in detail, each possible path she could take. Along the way, she continued to apologize for her confusion and indecision. In some ways, it seemed easier to just be told what to do and how to act. Carol continued to "check" to make sure that I wasn't annoyed and frustrated with her. By letting her repeat things and not telling her what to do or judging her, she was able to trust me completely. I respected her and her feelings. When she was "all over the place", I could still understand what she was feeling and repeat it right back to her. Doing so validated her. This helped Carol gain insight and finally "find" herself.

The multiple facets and dynamics of Carol's relationship with men could fill volumes, but I will attempt to summarize our many discussions. We began to analyze her newfound "love" with Bill. First of all, I thought it was very important to keep the relationship in perspective. I told her that she should keep in mind that this relationship with Bill was not "real" because each individual could easily choose the date, time, mood and intensity of almost every conversation. Each person could choose to reveal only the most appealing parts of him—or herself. Most people do not gain a complete picture of their loved one until they are living together. That is when all the "warts" show and relationships become more complicated.

Carol was initially appalled about my questioning her "love" for Bill. She felt that I may be trying to discount her intense feelings toward him and she started to get angry with me for the first time. "Aha," I thought. "This is a gift." For the first time, she was able to spontaneously express her feelings in a confrontational manner without hesitation or remorse. She trusted me enough to risk not being a "good" (automatically-agree-with-the-therapist) client. I acknowledged her dismay and let it go with the comment, "I just thought it was something you may want to consider."

As more weeks passed, we continued to discuss Carol's relationship with Bill. I continued to maintain impartiality about the relationship. I continued to listen to the many ways that this man had become important in her life. It was consistent and clear: He made every effort to listen to every emotional concern that she had raised. He gave her the time, unconditional love and attention that she craved. Bill was filling a need in Carol that Carl had not. A deep connection had been made—a connection of emotional intimacy that Carol had longed for all of her life.

She did not care that the setting was unreal and that their time was limited to the best moments they had to share. This was it. This was the unconditional love she would no longer live without. From now on she would accept no less from any man.

Now it was time to focus on Carol's anger toward Carl. She came to realize that she had primarily established a codependent relationship toward her husband. Because of Carl's problems with alcohol and Carol's fear of his mood changes, (which could possibly lead to a relapse), all of her needs were automatically subservient to his needs. She easily adopted this position since it was so familiar and similar to the "pride" she had felt "holding the family together" while growing up. But now she would not be so accepting of this newly clarified role. In fact, her emotional survival depended on it. Little by little, week by week, Carol and I would role— play conversations that were long overdue between her and her husband.

At first, Carl complained to his wife that she was "getting too sensitive," that she was "over-reacting" or that she "must be getting her period." But for the first time, Carol would not back down. She knew from her conversations with me, (as well as her conversations with Bill), that her needs and feelings were very important and each issue needed to be addressed. Carl knew that his wife was serious about her expectations and he started responding to her feelings like he never had before. New lines of communication were being established. Carol was also surprised to see that Carl's behavior was changing toward her, although Carl himself was not in therapy. Carol's confidence in expressing her feelings and her newly empowered attitude was creating a healthy change in her spouse and a welcome reawakening to their marital relationship.

At the same time, Carol continued enjoying her time with Bill. But over time, the nature of her relationship began to shift. Her love for Bill remained very strong, but she started to feel less "grateful" and "desperate" for the recognition and validation she had always deserved. She no longer dwelled on each minute she could find to spend with Bill. Sometimes she even preferred to eat lunch all by herself.

Carol started to find love where she most needed it: within herself. She began to love herself as the bright, sensitive and compassionate person she has always been. She even became better at accepting compliments from family, friends and co-workers without stating, "Oh, it's nothing." The whole experience had been heart-wrenching and soul-searching. Talking about where to find love had meant trying to overcome a life filled with fear, shame, and others' expectations.

Did Carol stay at the job? Did she stay married? Did she continue her relationship with Bill? Do you want to judge what was in her best interest? In the end, it could only be Carol's decision to find her love and choose the best path.

Life Is a Bitch and Then You Die: Growing, Evolving, and Discovering the Real Meaning of Your Whole Life

When I reflect on my life, including all the history and the hardships, I always end up looking back to the past generation or two. My mother was born Mary Kathryn Sullivan of Irish descent. She was raised as an only child who never knew her biological father. My mother told me that she was raised with a stepfather. "But," she added, "my mother told my stepfather to leave before I was eleven and I haven't seen him since."

My mother always described her mother as having always been very cruel and abusive toward her. "She always made me call her by her first name when we were out in public," she added, "because she didn't want other men to know she had a child."

My mother admitted that part of the reason she married Bill Harrell, her first husband, was to get out of her mother's house. She and Bill had two children,

Gerry and Lynne. Bill later died from complications after suffering from injuries during World War II. While still in her twenties, my mother was widowed with two children. She didn't get along with her mother and she had very few people to help her, either financially or emotionally. She was a "Lost Soul."

My father, Irving Scheinberg, was of Austrian/ Polish heritage. He was raised a Jew, though he never spoke much about it. He was the youngest of eight children, but he was closest to only one brother, "Eli." Unfortunately, Eli died suddenly in his twenties from a brain aneurysm.

My father never talked about his upbringing, but my mother once told me that his father was "very slow, probably mentally retarded" and an alcoholic. My father's mother was so distant that she didn't even keep in touch with him after he entered the armed services. It was an older sister, "Aunt Sylvia," who took my father in after the war. My father was a stern, quiet man who worked seasonally as a carpenter. He was also a "Lost Soul."

My mother and father never got along with each other. The only period of time that I recall them acting somewhat in love with each other was when I was about two or three years old; rare images of a hug and a kiss still reside deep in my memory. I always wondered why these two Lost Souls would marry in the first place. Just a few years ago, my mother finally told me the truth.

As part of my own personal growth, I had allowed a professional hypnotherapist to help me get into a deep trance state. In a regression to earlier and earlier ages of experience, I recovered what appeared to be memories of my actual birth! Feeling very excited, but somewhat skeptical at the same time, I called my mother in Florida to corroborate my recollection. In fact, my memory did prove to be accurate! The conversation was a perfect segue to asking my mother how she and my father got together in the first place.

Initially, they were introduced through a mutual friend. Then they ended up dating for a few months.

"But how did you decide to get married?" I asked.

"Oh, we just decided," Mom replied evasively.

"What do you mean? How did you decide?" I prompted.

After several minutes, my mom finally admitted, "I missed my period."

My Mom was pregnant with me. I knew that this must have been very difficult for her. She already had two children and now she was pregnant with a third child outside of marriage. Back in the 50's, this was a very difficult predicament.

"So how did you deal with that?" I continued.

"Well, I didn't know what to do," she admitted.

Knowing that she was partially dependent on her own abusive mother, I probed further.

"What did your mother say?"

"I didn't tell her."

"Why not?"

"Because I was afraid that if she found out, she would have had my children taken away from me for being an unfit mother."

"Why would she do that?"

"Because she wanted them. She didn't care so much about Lynne. After all, she never liked little girls. But she really wanted Gerry."

"That's crazy," I responded. "What did you do?"

Mom started becoming evasive again, but I pressed on. I had to know. "I realize it must have been a very difficult situation for you. I realize that you probably weren't ready to have another baby... I know you and Dad didn't know each other that long... So what did you do?"

There was silence on the other end of the phone.

"Listen Mom, you can tell me anything now. It's okay. It's in the past... I can handle anything you have to say."

"Well... I went to the doctor," Mom began, "and I asked him for something to bring on my period. So he gave me some pills to take."

"And then what happened?"

"I spotted a little bit, but nothing more."

"And what did Dad say about the whole thing?"

"When I realized that I was going to have another

baby, he said he would do the 'right' thing."

"Marry you?"

"Yes."

Quickly, a small wedding was planned. The ceremony was conducted by a justice of the peace in a small apartment. A few friends and relatives attended.

Seven months later, my mother gave birth to me. It was just as I had remembered. Initially, I looked and felt healthy. But I did not nurse properly. Mom's breast milk spilled from my nose. Upon closer examination, the doctor discovered that I was born with a partial cleft palette extending from the roof of my mouth to the tip of my uvula- (the piece of flesh that hangs down toward the throat and is necessary to be able to swallow properly). My mother now admitted to me a long kept secret: "I always thought that the pills I took probably caused you to have this birth defect."

"That's okay, Mom," I reassured her. "It doesn't make any difference now."

My corrective surgery would have to wait until I was old enough to tolerate it, at approximately two-and-a-half.

I am lucky enough to be able to remember my first few years on this Earth. I remember Mom making it very clear that I was loved very much. There was always a special "look" that she gave me at certain moments of the day, which felt very good. In those first years, I know we had a strong, loving "connection" to each other.

When I was two-and-a-half and talking constantly, like most children at this age, it became time for my surgery. In 1955, no one told mothers how to prepare themselves or their children for such a traumatic event. Mothers were told to leave their children at the hospital and not worry about their child's screams as they walked away. The doctors would take care of everything. They would restrain a child from acting out of control and they would medicate him or her to fight fears of abandonment. Mom always said that her relationship with me was never the same after that day.

Two weeks later, I clearly remembered that my throat was healing and I had tried to talk without my throat hurting too much. "I'm thirsty. I want some water," I had tried to say.

"What, honey?" Mom responded.

"I'm thirsty. I want some water," I repeated.

"What did you say?" Mom asked again.

I did not realize that all the sounds were coming out differently.

"I want water," I persisted sadly.

"What was that?"

"Water," I said once more, pointing toward the kitchen.

"I'm sorry. I don't know what you're saying," said Mom regretfully. She watched as I gradually climbed atop the kitchen cabinets, reached for my cup, and tried to fill it with water, all by myself. This became an early lesson in not depending on anyone else. There would be repercussions, both good and bad.

Another year passed, and at three years of age, I realized that Mom and Dad were drifting apart as well. I couldn't put it into words, but I could feel the tension between them. The way they looked and talked to each other changed a lot. And they hardly ever hugged or even touched each other anymore. They argued and made up, argued and made up, month after month, year after year.

By the time I was nine, weeks would go by without Mom and Dad talking to each other. But by now I had two younger brothers, Mark (age six) and Dale (age three). My older sister, Lynne, would often let Mom sleep late. She was good at being the "second mother" who would help all of her younger brothers get dressed and ready for school.

I remember that Lynne would love to comb my hair in the latest slicked-down, Brylcream-assisted style. We would argue frequently about which side my hair would be parted on and whether it should be brushed to the side or straight back. It was a special kind of love shared by a nine-year-old boy and his sixteen-year-old sister.

Soon Lynne decided to double up on her high school classes so she could finish school before her seventeenth birthday. Lynne knew how to take care of others very well, so she naturally chose to attend Nursing School at Queens General Hospital in New York City. Our older brother, Gerry, was seventeen years old and he was soon to finish high school himself.

Mom and Dad continued to struggle with each other and with the rigors of parenthood. They didn't seem able to agree on anything, but they continued to work hard in order to pay the bills. And they never went to bed at the same time. Though everyone was busy heading in different directions, the tension in the household was inescapable. I heard my dad's voice getting angrier and louder, and sometimes he broke things in the house. It was also clear that my mom was becoming more and more fearful and depressed.

At the same time, Dad was having a hard time keeping up with the bills. He was an assembly line worker at Grumman Aircraft Company and he had to work as much overtime as the company would offer. Sometimes Dad would work seven days a week for two months at a time. That's how he showed his love for his family—by "keeping a roof over our heads and food on the table"—something he could not depend on when he was growing up. I did not recognize or appreciate this as love at the time because I was preoccupied with keeping a safe distance.

I knew how to take care of myself. I did not ask for anything from Mom or Dad. And when Dad got angry and Mom grew very quiet, I helped Mark and Dale stay out of the line of fire.

When I was ten, I overheard many calls from Lynne to Mom and Dad. She accused them of cashing her "Survivor Benefit" checks that came to the house after her father died from World War II injuries. She accused them of many other things of a very private nature. Mark, Dale and I knew not to ask any questions. We knew how to stay safe. When the phone calls ended, Dad told Mom and my brothers and I never to see or talk to Lynne ever again. At seventeen, my sister Lynne was considered "dead" to the family.

This was the Scheinberg family. This was my family. For me, this was a childhood I hated. (And these are just the "highlights".) I learned not to trust. I learned not to talk. I learned to stay outside the family "battlefield," where I could observe vigilantly and prepare my defense silently. My family was "boot camp" for a child who felt unloved, at least at that time. My family was too much of a war zone for me to realize that in spite of the chaos, my Mom and Dad actually loved me very much. I couldn't feel that until much later.

At eleven years of age, I began to enter adolescence. My father started to look at me a little differently. "Come here, I want to talk to you," he said, with a very stern look on his face.

I suddenly felt very nervous. My mind began to race. A stream of thoughts crossed my mind: "I don't think I did anything wrong... Could there be anything I overlooked? I always made sure I was a good boy... Would he hit me anyway?"

I followed him as he walked into my room and shut the door behind me. I was frozen in fear.

"You're at an age when I can start talking to you about certain things," Dad proceeded to say.

I didn't know what he was talking about, but I continued to listen carefully.

"Me and your mother are thinking about getting divorced, so I thought I could have a talk with you so you could tell me what you think about it."

"What?" I thought. "I guess I'm not in trouble. But I wouldn't dare say anything. What if I said the wrong thing? He would kill me."

I looked up for a moment and my eyes met Dad's. He was actually trying to talk to me as another person, but I couldn't look at him in the face. I was too terrified of him and that wasn't about to change now. My silence became quickly uncomfortable for both of us. I had to say something.

"Well, I don't know," I mumbled, glancing up at those big dark eyes one more time, then quickly redirecting my gaze back at the floor.

Dad didn't know what else to say. The silence was more than he could bear, also. Then he just got up and left me alone in the room. Where I could feel safe once again.

In the days that followed, I overheard many, many arguments and then dead silence. No one else was leaving this house. Unfortunately, my parents didn't make enough money so that either one of them could afford to leave the house. We would all have to just deal with it.

Months later, Mom's friends plotted a separation once again. A woman we called "Aunt Marge" wanted to help Mom force the issue in some kind of sneaky way. I didn't know what was happening, but one day Marge took Mom, Mark, Dale and me to her house to live. It was irrational and confusing, but I knew not to ask any questions. I overheard Marge coaching Mom about how to get alimony and child support, and at age eleven I knew what that meant... She soon turned to coach me: "When the judge asks you which parent you want to live with, what are you going to say?"

"Oh no," I thought. "I don't want any part of this." I kept quiet and safe.

But Marge persisted, "You have to tell me. What are you going to say? What are you going to say?"

I thought about it very carefully. Maybe I could answer. After all, I couldn't imagine that Mom or Marge would hit me very hard if I gave them the wrong answer. Marge was a stranger to me. And Mom was emotionally weaker than I was. She was worn down and very depressed. I hadn't seen her smile in months. I didn't know what she was thinking. She was lifeless. In fact, I didn't feel a connection to her at all.

On the other hand, I always knew exactly how my father felt, even if he was scary. He was forthright and painfully honest. I knew how to stay out of his way when he was angry and I appreciated his subtle nod of approval when I completed my chores around the house. I felt bad for Mom, but she confused me. At eleven years old, I knew that my place was with my father.

"I want to be with my father," I blurted out.

"What?" Marge screamed. Then she turned to my mother and asked, "What's the matter with him?"

Mom remained quiet and just shrugged her shoulders. I was never asked that question again.

The following week, with no further discussion or explanation, we all returned home.

In the years that followed, I would go to school, go to my part-time job and then return home. I sold seeds, then greeting cards and then I found a great job serving soda at a movie theatre.

When I went home, I checked on my brothers and then secluded myself in my room. I listened to lots of music. I loved the rebellious tales of "hard rock" and "heavy metal." I also identified with Simon and Garfunkel's songs of loneliness and isolation. "The Sound of Silence" touched a deep nerve inside of me.

"I Am a Rock" was my badge of courage: "...a rock feels no pain, an island never cries."

But Jim Morrison and Jimi Hendrix died along with John Kennedy and Martin Luther King. Nixon and Johnson were sending more troops to Viet Nam. I watched soldiers being killed every night on the news. I saw pictures of Vietnamese women and children being burned alive with napalm.

There was war and hardship in my home as well. My youngest brother, Dale, took the place of my sister as the "troubled" child in the family. He was very bright, but he always misbehaved in school. Sometimes my mother would keep this a secret. But then she started complaining to my dad.

It was painful to hear my brother being beaten almost every night. My father thought it was his duty. He had been brought up to think that this was the only way to teach a child a lesson. As I heard Dale's screams, I thought that there must be a way to intervene to stop this madness. But I dared not confront my father or this big man would beat me too.

One day, my father decided to talk to me once again:

"What's the matter with that kid? Why doesn't he ever learn? It's gotten to a point where he just expects to be beaten every night. It just doesn't make a difference to him."

This was my opening. "Let me talk to him," I replied.

Being careful not to elaborate or direct any criticism toward my father, I continued, "I think if I can just talk to him I can help him figure it all out."

"Okay, it's up to you," Dad replied.

My brother Dale became my first "client." I learned quickly how to make every effort to mediate this explosive situation on a daily basis. I was able to help stall many more beatings with keen observation, quick analysis and intervention. "Okay, I'll talk to him," I would constantly reassure my father. "I think he'll be better," I hoped. It was up to me to use my words to make the violence stop.

After finding my role and purpose in my family, they didn't seem so bad after all. The turmoil never ended, but I tried to stay outside the battle lines and the controversies. I only entered the family to give advice and then leave. I always returned to my room, my safe haven.

Only from a distance was it safe to feel loved. Though the word "love" was never mentioned, I studied my parents' actions to see what I could discern: My mother never felt loved, either by my father or by her own mother. She was spiritually lost and eternally depressed. She had no love for herself and little to offer. But she tried to give me all she had.

My father didn't know what love was either. He was the youngest of eight children. His sister, Sylvia, was the only sibling who cared for him and one of the few relatives I ever met on either side of the family. (I never knew my grandparents.)

The only way my father could show his love for me was through work. When I was sixteen, he never hesitated giving me a ride to and from my part-time job at the movies, though I knew he was often very tired. When I was seventeen, he would work on my old Buick all day on his only day off from work in order to help me keep it running.

At seventeen years of age, I also continued to do a little social work with my family while keeping my personal needs and feelings buried deeply. My peers were part of the anti-war protests, doing drugs and forming communes. The Beatles were singing "All You Need is Love." Another part of my psyche began to take root. The idea of leaving the hurt and anger buried and following idealistic notions of "Peace and Love" captured my imagination and helped me survive my pain. At seventeen, I was confused and dying inside. I was also dying to find love and feel loved. It would always take awhile to try to clear my mind so that I could fall asleep at night.

"Wake up!" my fourteen-year-old brother yelled.

"What?" I responded, awakened abruptly out of my deep sleep.

"Can you take me and my friends to the beach?" Mark asked.

"No, I'm sleeping," I replied.

"Oh, c'mon. Please?" he persisted.

I awoke to a beautiful, sunny day. It was a good day to go to the beach.

"How many friends are you talking about?" I asked Mark. My fourteen-year-old brother had lots of friends. He had learned to never be at home. He was one of the most outgoing, sociable and popular kids at school.

"I think only about four," he replied.

My '61 Buick Electra was running again. My father helped me seal the radiator with some epoxy he had brought home from work so I could drive it for a whole day without the water leaking out. Counting me, Mark, and four friends, we could easily fit into the monster and make the ten-minute drive to the beach.

Once we arrived, I carefully unloaded my blanket, laid down and planned to go back to sleep. My brother and his friends ran off to the water, but one of the girls, "Gerry," remained with me and began to ask me about my car. I soon found myself engaged in a long conversation about how far I wished to drive now that my car was "fixed." My dream for the summer was to be able to drive all the way to the easternmost end of Long Island.

"I want to get all the way out to Montauk," I said with great excitement.

"That sounds great," replied Gerry. "Let me know when you're going and I'll go with you."

I thought, "She seems very nice but she's one of my little brother's fourteen-year-old friends... Could she be serious?"

I added, "You would? What do you think your mother would say if you asked her?" After all, I couldn't imagine any mother of a fourteen-year-old girl would feel comfortable letting her daughter go on a long day trip alone with a seventeen-year-old guy whom she had never met.

"Oh, she'll be fine," Gerry responded with confidence and a smile.

"Who is this girl?" I thought. We continued to speak for hours on the beach. As a shy, quiet and confused young man, this was way out of character for me. I enjoyed the day, but I couldn't understand what was happening.

On the way home, Mark and his friends piled back into my car. But this time, Gerry had made it a point to sit in the front bench seat right next to me. I was nervous. I tried to ignore any feeling welling up inside me. As I pulled the car out of the parking lot and onto the highway, Gerry proceeded, ever so gently, to pick up her left hand and rest it upon my right leg. My breath stopped and my heart pounded. I could not respond.

When we got back to my house, I casually said my goodbyes to all of my brother's friends. Most went on their way, but Gerry stayed behind. Looking at me straight in the eye, she asked, "So are you going to call me when you go to Montauk?"

I took a deep breath, and I could not look away from the soul beneath those big brown eyes. "Yeah, sure," I responded nervously. "I'll call you."

During the next year, through the end of my high school year, we were inseparable. We were as any two souls could be. But I could not put my feelings into words. Gerry was young in years, but she was light years older than I was emotionally. "I love you," she would say often.

"No, I don't think you really know what you're talking about," I would respond, since I was an emotional train wreck.

"I know how I feel," Gerry persisted. "And that's all there is to it."

I couldn't understand. No one had ever told me those words. "It doesn't make sense," I insisted. "I don't do anything for you." After all, the only recognition I got in my family was by helping someone. The only validation I got was by doing a good job.

"I just love you for who you are. You don't have to do anything and I'll love you anyway," Gerry insisted.

This was unreal to me. I was very scared. We had hours and hours of late-night talks. I cried a lot. Though often frustrated, Gerry's love never wavered. It took me over a year to understand the real meaning of pure, unconditional love.

My first year living away from home and attending college was highly conflicted. I was able to separate from the turmoil of the household and I could continue to find my own identity. I also dated many other women and experimented with the ideals of "free love" from the "hippie" counterculture. But as I was testing out new ideals and new social skills, I was also very lonely deep inside and I missed Gerry terribly.

In my sophomore year, I continued to test my ability to face adversity. It was important to my developing identity. The Viet Nam War was still raging and I waited to hear about my draft status. I was at risk of being pulled out of school and placed among those nightmarish images I had only seen on television. I was prepared to fight the draft if I had to.

Just before Christmas, in December 1972, I got a phone call. That was when I received the news that my sister, Lynne, had been murdered. Once again, I returned home and I became very quiet. Gerry was as loving and supportive as always, but I had returned to my survival mode. I did not cry at the wake or the funeral. My feelings were buried and my thoughts raced around in circles inside my head.

When I returned to college, my friends asked me if I was angry that Lynne had been senselessly killed. They told me that the whole situation seemed to be a mess and that I had every reason to be bitter.

"I can understand why people get bitter and angry,"

I replied. "But my sister was a kind and giving person who dealt with a lot of bad situations without being bitter or angry... I know that I have a choice about how to deal with all this and I don't think the answer is to be angry."

Throughout college and years later, I continued to grapple with many soul-searching issues. I made every attempt to open up to my best friend, Gerry, in the process. Sometimes I worked it out with resolution, sometimes I got stuck and became quiet and self-destructive.

Gerry and I were married in 1977. A year later, a series of events (described in the beginning of this book) caused me to fall back into a deep depression, which then led to my suicide attempt. Looking back, I believe that this event was one of the best days of my life—I needed a trauma to force me to lower my defenses and try to turn my life around (for the better). So in September, 1978 I began my healing journey in personal psychotherapy. I finished my graduate studies in 1981. We had our first and only child, Jared, in 1982. Each year continues to bring challenges, conflict, and ultimately greater insight and understanding. There are endless lessons to be learned, year-by-year, in each of our lives.

By the '90's, our marriage continued to grow and evolve. Gerry found herself leaning toward loving and teaching special-education students. I found myself loving the work of helping people to work out life's challenges. My private psychotherapy practice continued to grow until I could no longer find time to accommodate each caller. After many apologies to those in need and kindly suggesting that they seek help elsewhere, I decided (in 1993) to open a small mental health center. My passion to help and serve larger and larger groups of people continues to this day. My love and excitement about this work, and the deep personal gratification I feel *by helping people just like someone once helped me* is a mission that never ends.

During my early years, I thought of these traumas as irrefutable and insurmountable. But I have come through my journey with a new perspective. I now see all of these events as blessings. It is only through hard times that I have been prompted to do the deepest soul-searching. After all, when a person is coasting easily through life, he or she does not usually take the time to value or reassess his or her life. Thus it was with me. It has only been through adversity that I have been able to grow emotionally, evolve spiritually and discover the direction and meaning of my whole life.

It is my "Sacred Contract," (as Carolyn Myss might say), to take all that I have learned and pass it on to others through my practice of clinical social work. First I worked with individuals, then families and then large groups. My aim in writing this book is to pass on whatever knowledge and wisdom I have acquired to the family of humankind. This small contribution represents the direction, purpose and culmination of my life so far.

We are all connected by the very core of our existence. The glue that holds us together is pure, unconditional love. The higher self or universal consciousness that governs us all is God.

How you meet each challenge is always your choice. You can resign yourself to being victimized and remain stuck in one predicament or another for the rest of your life. And you can get depressed or stress yourself out in the process. Or you may choose to accept the challenge. If so, you need to do the work of being open and honest with yourself. Such is the School of Life.

If, for some reason, you choose not to work on being happy and gratified in life, I can appreciate and understand your reluctance. However, please know that your present problems won't go away without your help. They will resurface in some form or another throughout your life. So you'll have many opportunities to evolve and find the peace that is your true God-given nature. And that is what we all continue to strive for. It is our joint mission to turn all the traumas of our lives into a triumph of the spirit.

About The Author

Richard C. Scheinberg received his Bachelor's degree in Psychology and Sociology in 1975 from the State University of New York at New Paltz and his Master's degree in Social Work in 1981 from Adelphi University in Garden City, New York. He is currently a Licensed Clinical Social Worker in the state of New York and a Board Certified Diplomate in clinical social work by the American Board of Examiners in Clinical Social Work. Mr. Scheinberg served as an executive board member of the Suffolk County chapter of the Society of Clinical Social Work from 1984 to 1995. Because of his work with graduate students in the 1990s, Mr. Scheinberg was recognized as an Adjunct Assistant Professor at the New York University School of Social Work in January 2000.

Mr. Scheinberg is a psychotherapist with twenty-five years in private practice helping children, adults, couples and families is the director of Sunrise Counseling Center in Bay Shore, Long Island, New York, which he founded in 1993, and which now has a staff of fifteen clinical practitioners. Aside from being a human resources specialist for community organizations, employee assistance programs and managed care insurance companies, Mr. Scheinberg continues to serve as a seminar and workshop leader locally and as a business consultant outside of New York State.

Mr. Scheinberg has participated in many hours of professional development to enhance and advance his clinical repertoire of skills, including Certification in Hypnosis for Past Life Regression by the Dr. Brian Weiss Institute. Mr. Scheinberg also maintains an ongoing interest in mind-body and healing therapies; he is a certified Reiki practitioner and Reconnective healing practitioner.

Mr. Scheinberg has served on a clinical team in New York City Schools for the past twenty-five years, evaluating children and adolescents who are not functioning well in the classroom because they may have learning disabilities and/or emotional problems. He has also been available to work with many children in times of crisis. Mr. Scheinberg has also developed several pilot programs to enhance the education and emotional growth of children and their parents in New York City.

Mr. Scheinberg currently resides in Islip, New York with his wife of twenty-nine years, Geraldine. They have one son, Jared, who is now twenty-four years old.

For more information regarding Mr. Scheinberg and his work, please visit the author's website at **www.RichardCScheinberg.com** or contact him via e-mail at Richard@RichardCScheinberg.com.

Richard C. Scheinberg, Director
Sunrise Counseling Center
1555 Sunrise Highway
Bay Shore, New York 11706
Tel: (631) 666-1615
Fax: (631) 666-1709

Purchase Information

Further copies of this book may be purchased online via the author's website, AuthorHouse.com, Amazon.com, BarnesAndNoble.com, or Borders.com.

Printed in the United States
79778LV00001B/166-999